Flying
Hand-Launched
Gliders

John Kaufmann

Flying Hand-Launched Gliders

with drawings and diagrams by the author

Willam Morrow and Company
New York 1974

Printed in the United States of America.
2 3 4 5   78 77 76 75

Library of Congress Cataloging in Publication Data

Kaufmann, John.
  Flying hand-launched gliders.

  SUMMARY: Instructions for building, launching,
and flying model gliders. Includes suggestions for contest flying.
  1. Gliders (Aeronautics)—Models—Juvenile litera-
ture. [1. Gliders (Aeronautics)—Models] I. Title.
TL770.K36   629.133′1′33   73-17236
ISBN 0-688-20108-3
ISBN 0-688-30108-8 (lib. bdg.)
ISBN 0-688-25108-0 (pbk.)

The author wishes to thank
Mr. Robert Hatschek,
former U. S. team member
and second-place Wakefield winner,
World Free Flight Championships,
and Mr. Jack Minassian,
expert builder and contest flier,
for reading the manuscript of this book.

Contents

For my fellow Sky Scrapers

1

Getting Started

Something is circling in the sky. There are birds soaring, but it is no bird. Its wings, body, and tail are shaped from wood. It is a hand-launched glider. A boy runs across the field, chasing the glider as it drifts downwind. In a little while the boy walks back, ready to fly his glider again. He throws it hard. It whistles through the air, climbs high in a steep spiral, levels off, and starts circling slowly. But it does not come down. It keeps going up, soaring high and far on a strong, invisible current of rising air.

A hand-launched glider is a free-flight model airplane. Once you let it go, it is on its own. It flies without any control from wires, radio, or other device. Its only control comes from its own built-in design, from adjustments of its wings and tail, and from the way you throw it. It has no motor. Its only power comes from the force of your throw.

The glider has four main parts: the

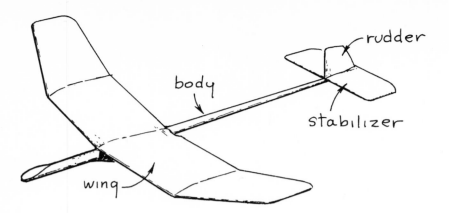

wing, the stabilizer, the rudder, and the body. The stabilizer and rudder together are called the tail. Each part serves a purpose and works with the other parts to make flight possible. The wing provides the essential force of lift that holds the glider aloft. The wing tips are raised to give the glider side-to-side stability, that is, to keep it from tipping over and being thrown off its flight path. The stabilizer controls and steadies the angle at which the wing meets the air, keeping the glider level and preventing it from nosing up or diving in wind gusts and other disturbances. The rudder aids the side-to-side stability. It holds the glider on a steady path, preventing tipping and keeping it from swinging left or right. The body holds the other parts in proper alignment with each other.

Building and flying hand-launched gliders is a great pleasure. They are the simplest kind of flying models, inexpensive to build, costing nothing to fly. They can be flown in wide country fields or in small city parks. Building them brings the satisfaction of craftsmanship, of shaping something carefully with your own hands. Flying them is a challenge to both mind and body. It involves a practical knowledge of flight, winds, and weather, as well as strong, skillful throwing and fast running.

Perhaps the greatest pleasure in flying a glider is to see it circling buoyantly in the air. Gravity keeps pulling down on it, but the glider seems to want to stay up as long as possible. The longer you can make your glider stay aloft despite the downward pull of gravity, the more exciting the flight is. Free-flight modeling is based on this idea of the long flight.

To stay up as long as possible, a glider must be light in weight. The wing creates lift to support the glider's weight as it moves forward through the air. The less weight the wing has to carry, the less quickly the glider will sink to the ground. Since almost all the weight of a hand-launched glider is in the wood itself, the wood has to be light. Gliders are made from balsa, one of the lightest woods. Balsa trees grow in certain tropical forest regions of Central and South America, particularly in Ecuador. Weight for weight, balsa is also one of the strongest woods. Thus gliders built of balsa are strong enough to

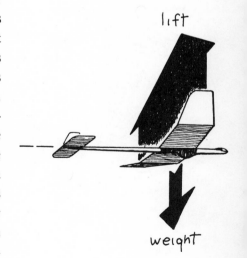

withstand the force of a hard throw, yet light enough to sink slowly in the glide. If you learn how to use this all-important material to best advantage, your gliders will be light, strong, and will stay up a long time.

Balsa comes in a wider weight range than any other wood. For example, white pine ranges from twenty-four to twenty-seven pounds per cubic foot. The lightest balsa weighs about four pounds per cubic foot (hence it is called four-pound wood), only one fifth as much as the heaviest balsa, which weighs about twenty pounds or more per cubic foot. The heavier the balsa, the greater its strength, so there is a wide range to choose from—very soft and light up to very hard and heavy.

When balsa trees are cut, grain structure lines can be seen on the ends of the logs. Rays extend outward from the central core of the tree and rings encircle the trunk. Boards are cut lengthwise from the balsa logs at certain angles to these structural lines and then cut into thin sheets. Cutting the boards at different angles to the tree's rays and rings gives the sheets certain types of grain, each with a different structural strength. The three principal types are called A-grain, B-grain, and C-grain.

Throwing a glider hard creates strong twisting and bending stresses in the thin

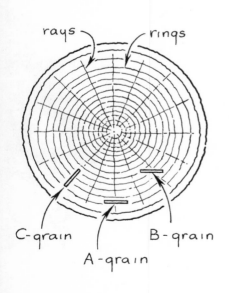

balsa flying surfaces, the wing and tail. C-grain, or quarter-grain, balsa has the greatest resistance to these stresses. C-grain sheets are cut along the ray lines, which gives them many plywoodlike grain layers for maximum rigidity with the least weight. Thin balsa surfaces have a tendency to warp out of shape after the glider is finished, changing the precise alignment of the wing and tail. C-grain wings and tails have maximum resistance to warping. To make stiff, lightweight, nonwarping flying surfaces, most expert builders prefer to use C-grain balsa whenever possible. True C-grain can be identified by the distinctive, large grain flecks running across the sheet.

C-grain

Although C-grain sheets are best for hand-launched glider wings and tails, they are hard to find in most hobby stores, especially in lighter weights. A-grain and B-grain sheets are the most common. A-grain sheets are cut along the ring lines around the trunk. The sheets are flexible and bend easily from edge to edge. Glider wings and tails made from A-grain balsa twist and bend more on launching and warp out of shape more easily than those made from C-grain. Lightweight A-grain sheets have a smooth, even appearance. Heavier weight sheets often have long, thin grain lines.

B-grain sheets are cut at various angles

A-grain

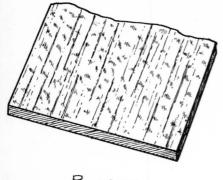

B-grain

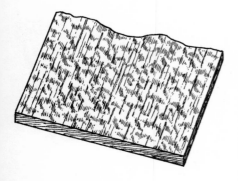

B/C grain

between the rings and rays. They are stiffer than A-grain sheets, but not as stiff as C-grain. Their appearance varies according to the angle at which they are cut. Some B-grain sheets look almost as even as A-grain and are fairly flexible. The stiffer sheets have mottled flecks that look almost like those of C-grain. These sheets are sometimes called B/C-grain and are very good for making wings and tails.

In most hobby stores, balsa is graded only by size, not by weight or grain. It is sold in sheets, strips, and blocks. Standard sheets are from 1/32 to 1/4 inch or more thick, 3 inches wide, and 36 inches long. Under each size you may find A-, B-, or C-grain, ranging from light to heavy in weight. Because sheets of all grains and weights are mixed together, it is important that you learn how to select the best pieces for your purposes.

Balsa sheets in hobby stores are usually eight-, nine-, or ten-pound wood, in A- or B-grain. Such wood is not the best for glider wings and tails; five- or six-pound C-grain would be much better. However, in order to get started building, just try to pick out the best pieces you can in the sizes required. Later you may want to order "contest" balsa by mail from a supplier, specifying the grain and weight you want. Then you must allow two weeks to order wood.

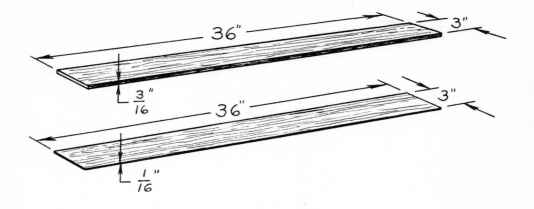

You will need one sheet in each of these sizes:

    3/16 by 3 by 36 inches
    1/16 by 3 by 36 inches

Examine the sheets for weight, grain, and straightness. First check the weight by the color. Balsa varies from almost white in the lightest grades to dark tan in the heaviest grades. So pick the lightest-colored pieces to get the lightest-weight wood. With practice, you can also tell a light-weight piece by the softer feel of its surface. Finally hold each one in your hand in turn to determine whether one is much lighter than the other. If you do not see or feel any real difference between two sheets, they probably weigh about the same.

Check the surface appearance for the type of grain structure. If you find two pieces that weigh about the same, one of A-grain and the other of B/C- or C-grain, choose the latter for stiffness. Make sure the grain is approximately the same throughout the sheet, not part A-grain and part B-grain. Sheets with markedly different grain tend to warp easily. Check for straightness of grain. The thin, light grain markings should run parallel to the edges of the sheet. Twist the sheet to check its stiffness.

Check the sheets for straightness. Hold each sheet by one end so that it hangs straight down and cannot bend with its own weight, as it would if you held it level. Look along the sheet from the side. It should be straight and flat. If a sheet is curved or twisted, don't buy it. In addition to the two sheets, buy a very hard strip of balsa 3/16 by 1/2 by 36 inches. If possible, try to get a piece with long, heavy grain lines. Check the straightness of the strip just as carefully.

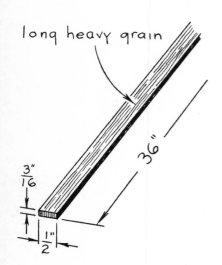

long heavy grain

$\frac{3''}{16}$

36"

$\frac{1''}{2}$

In addition, buy these items at the hobby store:

An X-Acto 35-ST Razor saw blade, 1 inch wide.

A small 45-degree right triangle.

A small bottle of sanding sealer.

A small bottle of thinner.

At a good hardware-paint store get:

A small bottle of Franklin Titebond glue. If not available, use Elmer's or a similar white glue.

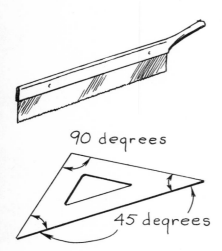

90 degrees

45 degrees

A tube of Duco cement.

One sheet of 3M Company "Production" sandpaper, 100 "medium" grade.

One sheet of 3M Company Wetordry Tri-M-ite sandpaper in each of these three grades: 240 "Very Fine," 320 "Extra Fine," 400 "Super Fine."

If you cannot obtain 3M sandpaper where you live, ask for one sheet each of the four grades in the best quality available.

A small, pointed, inexpensive paintbrush with soft hair.

A small pack of inexpensive, single-edge razor blades, the kind used for hobbies and paint scraping. (Also available at drugstores.)

A good quality 12-inch ruler.

A small amount of Plasticine clay.

At a lumberyard get:

A piece of 1-inch by 2-inch clear pine, 2 feet long. If you don't have an old table that can be cut, scraped with sandpaper, or dripped with glue, get a flat piece of board about a foot wide and a few feet long to work on.

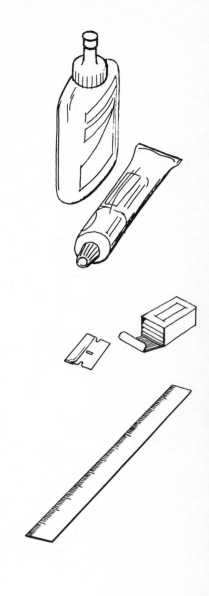

To shape the glider parts properly, you have to do a considerable amount of sandpapering, or sanding, as modelers call it.

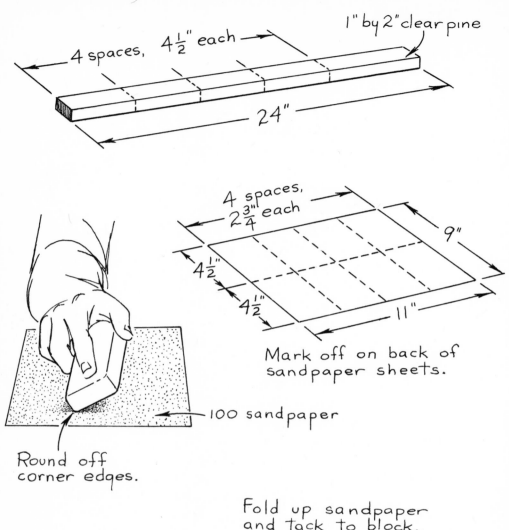

4 spaces, 4½" each

1" by 2" clear pine

24"

4 spaces, 2¾" each

9"

4½"

4½"

11"

Mark off on back of
sandpaper sheets.

100 sandpaper

Round off
corner edges.

Fold up sandpaper
and tack to block.

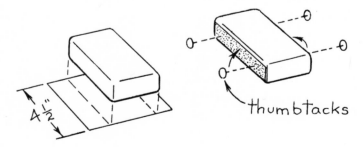

4½"

thumbtacks

The best method is to use sanding blocks. Make four blocks, one for each grade of sandpaper, using the 1-inch by 2-inch by 2-foot length of pine. Mark off 4½ inches four times and cut off the four pieces with a saw. Lay the 100 sandpaper on the work-table rough side up, and round off all the corner edges of the blocks by rubbing them against the sheet. Next, put the four sand-paper sheets, rough side down, on the table. Measure and divide them as shown. Cut out one small rectangle from each sheet with an old pair of scissors. Fold and tack the four pieces of sandpaper to the blocks as shown. Mark the tops of the blocks 100, 240, 320, and 400 so you can easily tell which is which.

Finally, tape a clean, smooth piece of extra heavy paper or thin cardboard, at least 8½ by 11 inches, to the corner of your work surface. Work on this paper, and keep it clean to prevent any rough spots from marring the soft surfaces of the balsa sheets.

2

Building
Your Glider

Right now you may think that building a glider is dull and tedious work, a necessary chore to be finished quickly so that you can get on to the excitement of flying. If so, you will probably be surprised to find that building is, in itself, a great pleasure. The shaped parts emerge beneath your hands from plain, flat pieces of wood. Finally the parts become the finished whole, and the glider seems eager to leave your hands and take to the air.

As a glider moves, billions of air molecules flow across its wings, body, and tail. If those parts are properly shaped and aligned, the air will flow smoothly and efficiently, making the glider fly as well as possible. But if the parts are poorly shaped or improperly aligned, the airflow will be disrupted and inefficient, and the glider's flight performance will suffer. Since good flying depends so much on good building, don't try to finish your glider in a hurry. The small details are crucial.

To build a glider, you use a three-view plan showing how it looks from the top, side, and front. A plan shows the wood sizes required, as well as the finished shape of the parts and how they are put together. However, to make your first glider, it will be easier to follow the step-by-step drawings in this book. You can copy the squared-off shapes of the wings and tail and draw them on your balsa wood. Measuring and laying out the parts is not difficult.

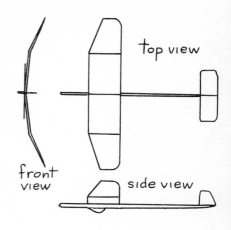

The Wing

Start with the wing. On your 3/16-by-3-inch balsa sheet, measure and mark 14 inches along one edge. Using your small right triangle, line up one side of the right angle with the edge of the sheet. Draw a line at right angles across the sheet at the 14-inch mark.

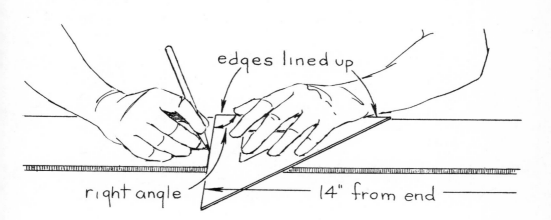

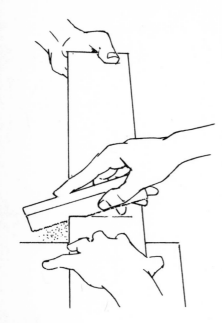

Now you are ready to cut through the sheet along the line with your saw blade. Put the sheet flat on the work surface with the 14-inch part extending out over the edge. Have someone hold the outer end of the sheet steady to keep it from breaking off as you finish the cut. Hold your saw blade at the angle shown. To start the cut, press lightly on the blade and pull it back toward you. In this way you will prevent the edge of the sheet from splitting. Then start sawing gently back and forth. Cut straight along the line. Go very carefully as you finish the cut, again to keep the edge of the sheet from splitting.

Measure and mark 7 inches from one end of the 14-inch piece. Draw a line across the sheet as you did before. This line, *C,* marks the center line of the wing. Do not cut it. Now measure 3½ inches both to the left and right of the center line. Draw lines *A* and *B* at right angles to the edge of the sheet. The wing tip is slanted back at the front, or leading edge. The rear, or trailing

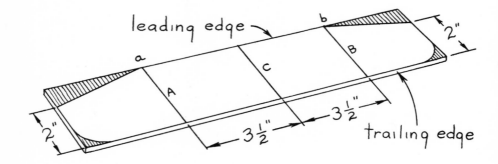

edge, is straight. To lay out the wing tips, measure 2 inches from the rear edge on each end of the 14-inch piece. Mark the points, then connect them with points *a* and *b* as shown. Remove the two corners with your saw blade by cutting them off just outside the lines. With your 240 sanding block, smooth and flatten the cut edges right to the lines. Then round off the rear corners of the wing tips.

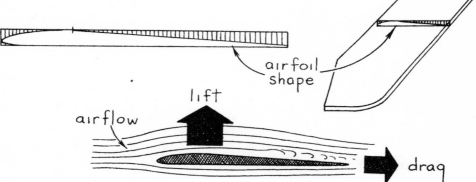

Now you have to shape the upper surface of the flat wing to give it a curved cross-section shape, or airfoil. The airfoil curvature is designed so that air, flowing across the wing, develops a lower pressure against the top surface than the bottom, thus causing the wing to lift. It is also designed to cause the least amount of drag, the retarding force that decreases lift and lessens the wing's efficiency. The airfoil's shape is important, so try to make it exactly as shown.

Trace.

First make two templates, or guiding shapes. Place a piece of tracing paper or thin tissue over the two template outlines. With a very sharp pencil, carefully trace both template shapes. Tape the tracing face down to a blank index card or some other smooth, stiff paper. Trace over the lines from the back. Remove the tracing paper and cut the templates with small, sharp scissors.

On your wing sheet, extend lines *A*, *B*, and *C* onto the reverse side from one edge to the other, using your right triangle to

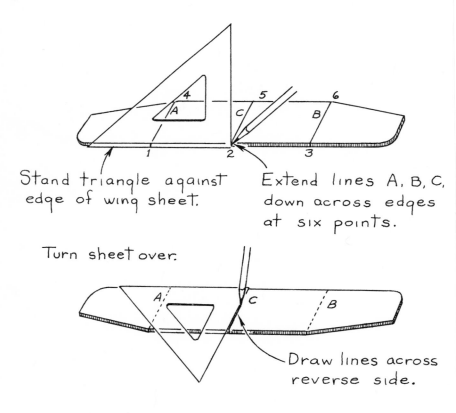

Stand triangle against edge of wing sheet.

Extend lines A, B, C, down across edges at six points.

Turn sheet over.

Draw lines across reverse side.

be sure they are straight. Lay the wing sheet down so that the surface you are now looking at will be the top of the wing. Measure and mark off ¾ inch from the leading edge along lines *A* and *B*. Pressing your sharply pointed pencil just hard enough to cut into the surface slightly, draw a line from the point on *A* to the same point on *B*. Pressing the line into the surface will keep it from disappearing when you start sanding. This is called the high-point line, since it marks the highest point on the airfoil curve.

Draw high-point line across top surface.

When you sand, keep these points in mind. To remove a lot of wood quickly at the start, use coarse sandpaper. Sand in circles and across the grain as well as in the direction of the grain. As you get down closer to the final shape, switch to a finer sandpaper, work more slowly, and sand along the length of the grain, not across it. That way you will not cut and weaken the outer wood fibers of the finished shape, as

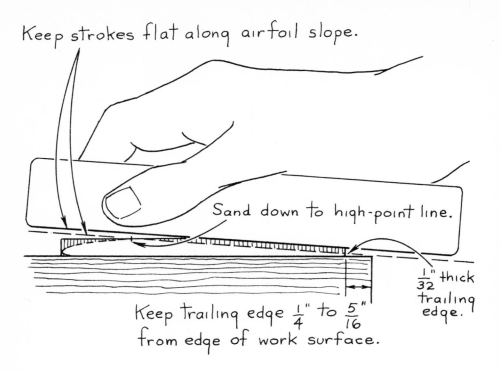

Keep strokes flat along airfoil slope.

Sand down to high-point line.

$\frac{1}{32}$" thick trailing edge.

Keep trailing edge $\frac{1}{4}$" to $\frac{5}{16}$" from edge of work surface.

you would if you sanded down all the way across the grain.

First using the 100 block, then with the 240 block, first sand the flat slope from the high-point line back to the trailing edge along the whole wing. Hold the trailing edge between one quarter and five sixteenths of an inch inside the edge of your work surface and parallel to it. This will prevent you from sanding the trailing edge too thin. Don't rock the sanding block. Keep all your strokes flat along the slope of the airfoil. When you get close to the high-point line, switch to your 320 block, and work lightly. When you stop sanding, the trailing edge should be about one thirty-second (which is half of one sixteenth) of an inch thick.

Next, sand the curved upper front section of the airfoil. Do the two inner panels first. Hold the leading edge even with the edge of the worktable to help keep your strokes straight along the wing. To check the airfoil shape as you sand, move the wing in from the edge of the table and fit airfoil template number *1* against it as shown. Again start with the 100 block, then the 240 block. Switch to the 320 block when you get close to the final shape. Don't sand away the high-point line. Keep sanding until the template fits snugly along

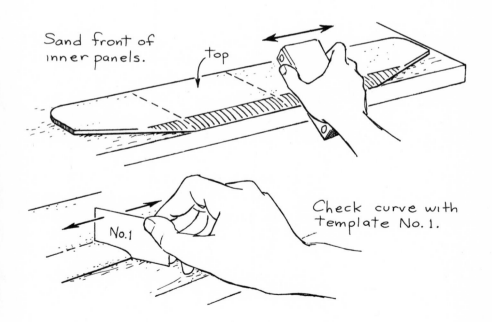

Sand front of inner panels.

top

Check curve with template No. 1.

No. 1

the curve from the high-point line to the leading edge. Now curve the underside of the leading edge of the inner panels to complete the airfoil shape. Use airfoil template number *2* as shown to check the curvature of the underside of the leading edge.

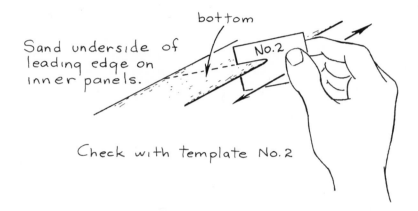

Sand underside of leading edge on inner panels.

bottom

No.2

Check with template No. 2

The wing tips taper in width from 3 to 2 inches. Their thickness also tapers, from 3/16 inch to about 1/16 inch at the tip end. Using your 240 sanding block, taper the thickness with a slight curve as shown. The high-point line slants back to a point ½ inch behind the leading edge at the tip ends. Measure and mark these points, and draw the high-point lines on both wing tips.

Sand the wing-tip airfoil shape by extending the shape of the center panels, gradually thinning the wing toward the

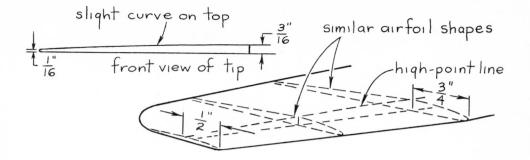

slight curve on top

$\frac{3''}{16}$

similar airfoil shapes

$\frac{1''}{16}$

front view of tip

high-point line

$\frac{3''}{4}$

$\frac{1''}{2}$

end of the tip. Since the airfoil template will not work here, shape the tip airfoil as carefully as you can by eye. A bright light slanting from the side is very helpful when you sand a shape without a template. By turning the shaped piece at different angles to the light, you can easily detect bumps, flat spots, or depressions that are much harder to see in a direct overhead light. Finally, sand the whole wing lightly with your 400 block to smooth the surfaces.

The wing panels must be cut apart and glued at the proper angles. The angle in the center is called the dihedral angle. Straight wings having only the center angle are called dihedral wings. Wings such as this kind, with separate wing-tip panels angled up, are called polyhedral wings. The edges joining the wing panels are called breaks.

To cut the wing panels apart, first draw the three break lines across the top surface. If the marks on the leading and trailing edges are no longer visible after the sand-

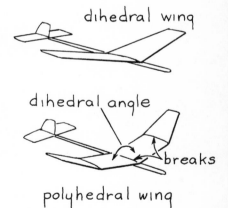

dihedral wing

dihedral angle

breaks

polyhedral wing

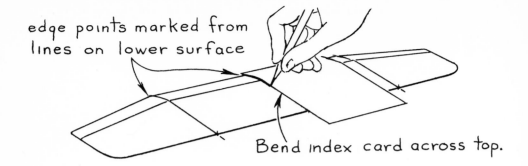

edge points marked from
lines on lower surface

Bend index card across top.

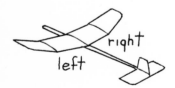

right

left

ing, mark them again from the lines on
the lower surface. Use a straight-edged
piece of index card or thin cardboard to
draw the lines. Bend the card across the
top surface and line it up with the marks.

Hold the wing flat side down on the
worktable, with the line to be cut extending past the edge. Saw about one-quarter
inch through the thin trailing edge first
by pulling the blade gently toward you.
Now cut across from the leading edge. To
make sure the cut is straight up and down,
don't tilt the saw blade. Have someone
hold each panel so it does not break off
near the end of the cut. Mark *L* (Left) and
R (Right) on two small pieces of tape. Put
them on the two center panels so you can
tell which is which. The left and right
sides of a wing or a model are located by
looking at it from the rear.

To sand the breaks to the correct angles,
first make the two angle templates shown,
the same way you made the airfoil template. Mark the templates "center break"
and "tip break." Sand the break angles on
the inner panels. Put the panel on the

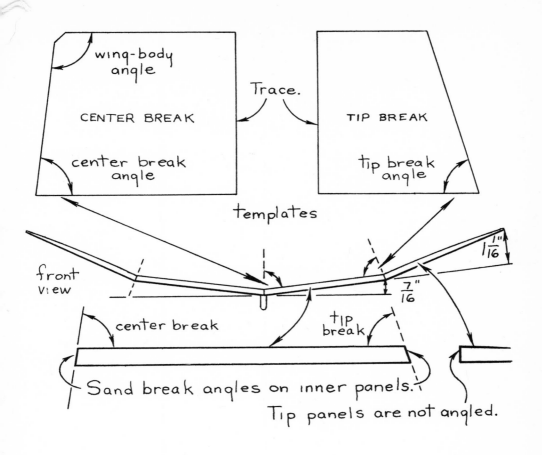

wing-body angle

CENTER BREAK

center break angle

Trace.

TIP BREAK

tip break angle

templates

front view

$1\frac{1}{16}''$

$\frac{7}{16}''$

center break

tip break

Sand break angles on inner panels.

Tip panels are not angled.

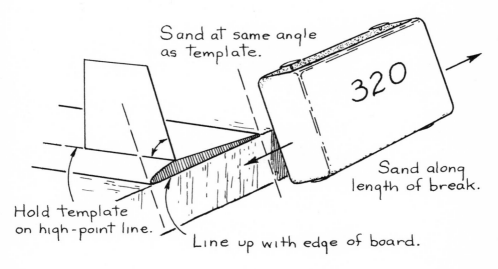

Sand at same angle as template.

320

Sand along length of break.

Hold template on high-point line.

Line up with edge of board.

work surface flat side down with the break extending out to the edge. Place the proper template next to the break as shown. Tilt your 320 sanding block to the same angle as the template and sand gently and gradually. The edge of the worktable will help keep your sanding strokes straight across the entire break.

Now glue the panels together. Work very carefully, since it is practically impossible to correct these glue joints without damaging the wood once they have dried. To prevent the wing from sticking to the workboard, do the gluing on a piece of plastic food wrap about twelve inches square, taped down at the corners. To make the glue joints as strong as possible, always use a first coat of Titebond or white glue thinned with water. This mixture penetrates much deeper into the wood grain than the normal thicker glue. Mix a tablespoon of glue and the same amount of water in a small jar. Brush a coat on all the break edges. Let the thin glue soak in and set for about fifteen minutes.

Glue each wing tip to each inner panel first. Cover the two edges of each break evenly with a thin coat of regular strength glue. Put each inner panel down on the plastic. Weight it with a small heavy object such as a pair of pliers resting on a piece of scrap wood. Push the tip panel up against the other panel. Tilt the tip panel and prop it up exactly 1 1/16 inches from the table surface with a piece of scrap wood. Wipe away the excess glue, and smooth off the joint by running your wet fingertip along it.

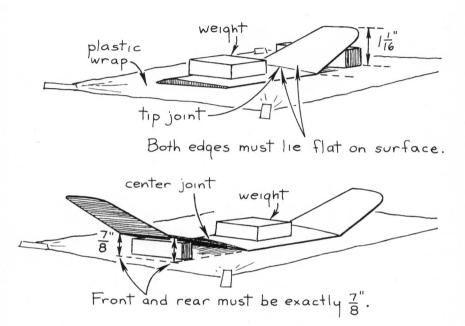

Both edges must lie flat on surface.

Front and rear must be exactly $\frac{7}{8}$".

After the two halves of the wing have dried for about two hours, glue them together along the center break. Keep one inner panel flat, and weight it down. Prop up the other tip break exactly ⅞ inch. Check to make sure that the center edges of both inner panels are perfectly flat against the table. Also make sure that both the leading and trailing edges of the raised inner panel are exactly ⅞ inch above the table. This will insure that the wings are set together evenly.

The Body

The body will be made from your 3/16-by-½-inch strip of hard balsa. Start by cutting a 14½-inch piece from it. Next, measure along the edge 2¾ inches, 3 inches beyond that, 7 inches beyond that, and 1⅝ inches. Mark points *a,b,c,d,e* as shown. Measure ¼ inch across the strip from point *a*. Mark the point and connect it to point *b* with a curving line as shown. Using your 100 and 240 blocks, sand the edge of the strip down to the line.

The wing will be attached to the body between points *b* and *c,* the stabilizer between *d* and *e*. Both the wing and the stabilizer must be set exactly flat on the same horizontal line. To be sure this alignment is correct, first check to see that the upper edge of the body between points *b* and *e* is flat. Place the straight edge of your ruler along the top edge of the body. Hold them up toward a window or a light. Does any light show under the ruler between points *b* and *e*? If so, does it show under the ends or the middle? If light shows under either or both ends, sand the center lightly between points *b* and *e* with your 320 block. If light shows under the

center, sand both end portions lightly.
Sand gradually and keep checking until
the ruler lies flat along the edge with no
light showing. Go easy on the sanding here.
Only a slight amount may be needed to
make the edge flat and level.

Lay out the side shape of the body.
Measure 7/16 inch down from points *b*
and *c* as shown, to locate and mark points
bb and *cc*. Draw a line through the points
to locate the nose point *aa*. Measure ¼
inch down from point *d* and mark point
dd. Connect points *cc* and *dd*. Measure
1/16 inch down from point *e* and mark
ee. Connect points *dd* and *ee* with a slight
curve as shown. Using your 100 and 240

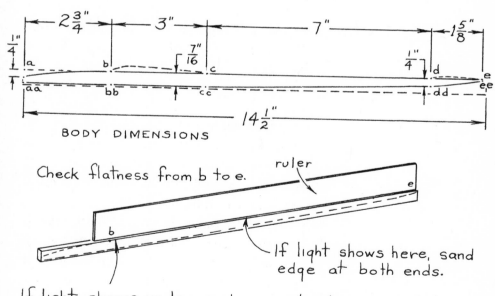

BODY DIMENSIONS

Check flatness from b to e.

ruler

If light shows here, sand edge at both ends.

If light shows under ends, sand edge in middle.

BODY
CROSS-SECTION
SHAPES

From a to b

From b to c

From c to d

From d to e

blocks, sand the lower edge of the body to the lines you have just drawn.

With your 320 block, round off the upper corner edges of the body between points *a* and *b*, and between *c* and *d* only. Don't round the edges between *b* and *c*, or between *d* and *e*, where the wing and stabilizer will be glued to the body. You need all the flat area there to make a strong, solid glue joint. Round off the lower corner edges between *cc* and *ee*. Leave the bottom of the body flat between *aa* and *cc*.

The glue joint between the body and the wing has to be very strong to withstand hard throws and occasional crashes. Even thin glue does not penetrate thoroughly into very hard balsa, so it is a good idea to make a lot of small pinpoint marks on the body portion of the joint. They allow the glue to sink in deeper for a very firm grip. If, in a future glider, you use hardwood such as spruce for the body, be sure to pinprick it to allow for glue penetration. Next, check the underside of the center break to see if any excess pieces of glue have dried there. If so, sand them flat with your 240 block, to make sure the wing lies flat along the body.

Coat the underside of the center break with thin glue about one quarter of an inch out from the center line on both sides. Do the same to the top of the body between points *b* and *c*, and also about one eighth

of an inch down on both sides. Coating
these extra areas will make the joint even
stronger. After fifteen minutes, coat the
top edge of the body between *b* and *c* with
regular glue. Press the wing and body together. Seen from above, the wing must
be centered on the body at a right angle
to it. First make sure the center break is
in the center of the body. Then place your
right triangle against the trailing edge and
the side of the body as shown. If the angle
is 90 degrees as required, the triangle will
fit it exactly. If the triangle does not fit,
shift the wing slightly until it does. Hold
the wing as level as possible, and stick
three straight pins down through its center into the body as shown. Check to make
sure the alignment has not changed.

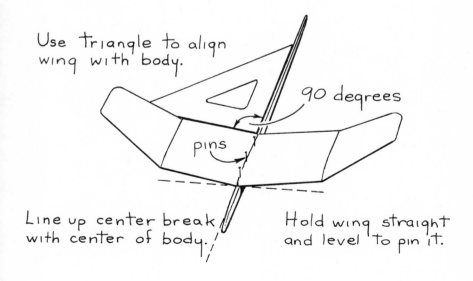

Use triangle to align
wing with body.

90 degrees

pins

Line up center break
with center of body.

Hold wing straight
and level to pin it.

While the glue is wet, place the glider upside down on the table, resting on its wing tips. Prop up the tail end so that the body is level. Run your fingertip along the joint on both sides to wipe off the excess glue. Next, use the center break template as shown to check the dihedral angle between the wing and the body. If the body is leaning to one side or the other, tilt it upright until the dihedral angle fits the template. The damp glue will readjust to the new position.

Let this joint dry for a couple of hours or overnight. When dry, put some extra glue where the wing leading edge meets the body. Smooth it off with a wet fingertip.

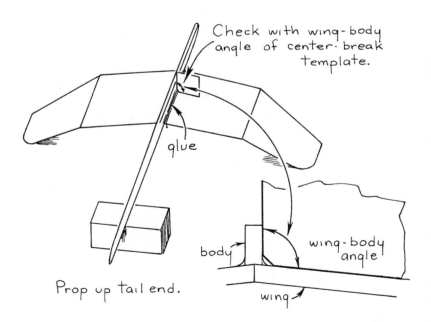

Check with wing-body angle of center-break template.

glue

Prop up tail end.

body

wing-body angle

wing

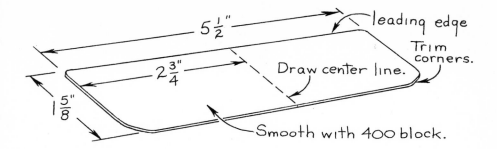

5½"
2¾"
1⅝"
leading edge
Trim corners.
Draw center line.
Smooth with 400 block.

The Stabilizer

While the glue is drying, you can start to make the tail. First cut the stabilizer from the 1/16-by-3-inch sheet. Mark off a length of 5½ inches, draw a line across at right angles, and cut it. You can cut this thinner sheet with a razor blade, but use a piece of cardboard underneath to keep from damaging your table. Measure and mark off 1⅝ inches across both ends of the piece from the same edge. Connect the two marks and cut along the line. Trim off the two corners as shown to complete the flat shape of the stabilizer. Smooth off one side by sanding it lightly with your 400 block. Locate the center line by measuring 2¾ inches from one end. Draw the line across at right angles. Place the sheet on the table with the smooth, marked surface down. The top will be the stabilizer's upper surface, which must be sanded to shape.

When you shape a thin piece like the stabilizer, hold it flat on the table with your fingertips. Press down firmly on the

SANDING THIN SHEETS

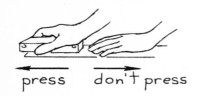

press   don't press

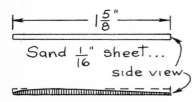

Sand $\frac{1}{16}$" sheet...

side view

to stabilizer airfoil shape.

front view

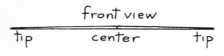

tip   center   tip

Taper thickness toward tips.

sanding block only on each forward stroke. To prevent the thin sheet from buckling up and snapping, don't press on the return stroke.

Using your 320 block, sand the upper surface to a thin airfoil shape, curving up and back, then tapering thinner at the trailing edge. Round off the leading edge as shown. Leave the trailing edge about half as thick as the wing's trailing edge. Taper the thickness toward the tips to save weight. Finally, smooth the upper surface with the 400 block.

Glue the stabilizer to the body. First, extend the center line up from the under surface over the leading and trailing edges. Measure and mark off 1 inch from the leading edge on the under surface center line. Place the glider on the table with the nose toward you. Prop up the body under the tail, so that the lower front of the body lies flat. Block up both sides of the wing to the same height. Put some weight on top of the wing to keep it from shifting. Use Duco cement on the stabilizer, since you may have to readjust it later. A white glue joint is difficult to loosen. However, you can readily dissolve a Duco glue joint with thinner, loosen or remove the stabilizer, then reglue it.

Spread a line of Duco cement along the inch you have marked off on the bottom center line of the stabilizer. Don't glue the

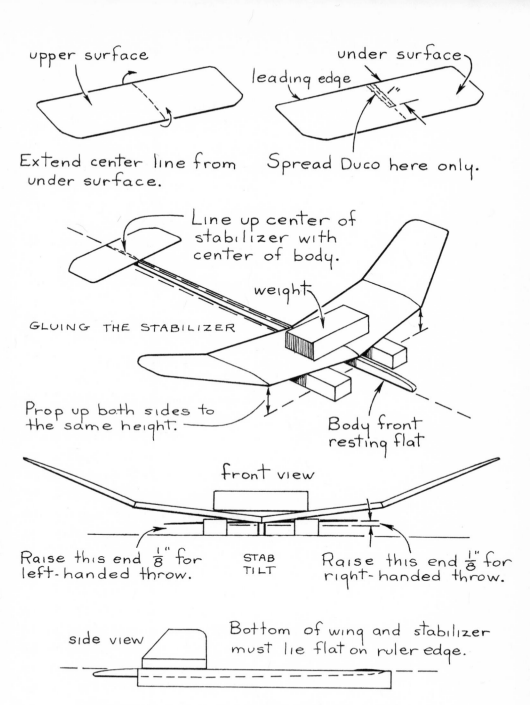

upper surface

under surface

leading edge

1"

Extend center line from under surface.

Spread Duco here only.

Line up center of stabilizer with center of body.

weight

GLUING THE STABILIZER

Prop up both sides to the same height.

Body front resting flat

front view

Raise this end ⅛" for left-handed throw.

STAB TILT

Raise this end ⅛" for right-handed throw.

side view

Bottom of wing and stabilizer must lie flat on ruler edge.

CHECKING THE WING- STABILIZER ANGLE

rear portion. Line up the center of the stabilizer with the center of the body, and press the two parts together firmly. Before the Duco dries, adjust the stabilizer tilt. Sight straight back from the nose. If you throw with your right hand, prop up the right end of the stabilizer (as seen from the front) so that its height above the table is ⅛ inch more than the left end. If you throw with your left hand, prop up the left end (as seen from the front) ⅛ inch higher than the right.

Now check from the side of the glider to make sure that the stabilizer is set level with the wing at exactly the same angle. Hold your ruler against the side of the body. The lower surfaces of both the wing and the stabilizer should lie flat against the ruler's edge. If you can see even a slight difference in the wing-stabilizer angle, remove the stabilizer by softening the glue joint with thinner. Then reglue the stabilizer so that it lies at the same angle as the wing, being careful to preserve the proper tilt.

The Rudder

Trace the rudder shape on the 1/16-inch sheet with the grain as shown. Cut it out with a razor blade. Sand the edges smooth with your 320 block. If you throw with your right hand, place the rudder down on the table as shown and sand it to a

rudder outline

Trace.

grain direction

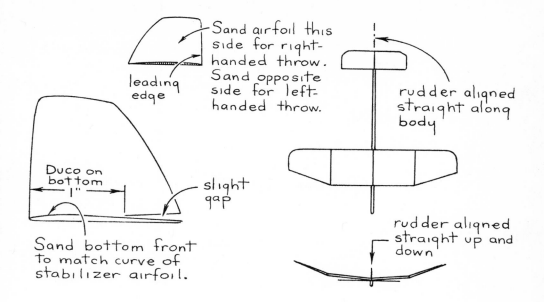

Sand airfoil this side for right-handed throw. Sand opposite side for left-handed throw.

leading edge

rudder aligned straight along body

Duco on bottom
1"

slight gap

Sand bottom front to match curve of stabilizer airfoil.

rudder aligned straight up and down

thin airfoil shape from front to back. If you throw with your left hand, put the rudder down on the opposite side, and sand the airfoil shape that way. Finally, sand the front part of the rudder's bottom edge to match the airfoil curve on the first inch of the stabilizer's top surface. Leave a slight gap between the rear part of the rudder and the top surface of the stabilizer.

To glue the rudder, coat the first inch of its bottom edge with Duco and press it onto the center line of the stabilizer. Before the joint dries, sight from directly in front of the glider. The rudder should be straight up and down, in line with the body. Only its thickness should show, not its side surfaces. Double-check from above and behind the tail; the rudder should line up straight down the center of the body. If it does not line up, adjust it to the correct position before the joint hardens.

The Finger Rest

Launching a glider requires a three-fingered grip. The index finger pushes forward on the wing next to the body, while the thumb and middle finger grasp the body underneath the wing. The finger rest at the wing-body joint absorbs the force of your throw and transfers much of the stress to the sturdy body rather than the thin wing. It also locates your index finger in the same position for each throw. Trace the outline on the 3/16-by-3-inch sheet with the grain as shown, and cut it out.

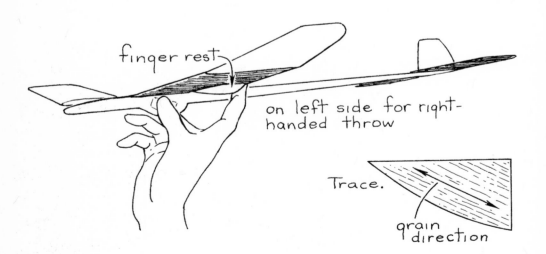

finger rest

on left side for right-handed throw

Trace.

grain direction

The finger rest is shown here on the left side for a right-handed thrower. A left-handed thrower would put it on the right side. However, some fliers prefer it the opposite way. If you have a strong preference, put the grip where you want it. If not, follow the plan. You can always change your mind later, put a finger rest on the opposite side, and sand off the first one.

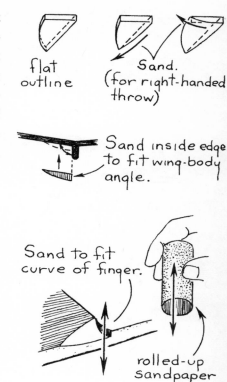

Shape the finger rest as shown, according to which side you put it on. Sand the inner edge to fit the dihedral angle between the wing and body. Smooth the curved surfaces with your 400 block. Use thin, then regular glue to attach it. This joint is important, so be sure to use enough glue. Hold the parts together firmly for about five minutes, and wipe away any excess glue at the edges. After the glue has dried for about an hour, roll an extra piece of 240 sandpaper into a tube ¾ inch in diameter. Use this to curve the rear edge of the finger rest and trailing edge as shown, so your index finger will fit comfortably but not too snugly when you throw.

The Throwing Grip

The throwing grip beneath the body allows your thumb and middle finger to hold the glider firmly when launching. Trace the outline onto the 3/16-by-½-inch

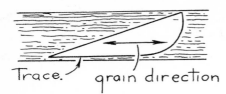

Trace. grain direction

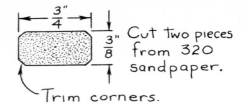

$\frac{3}{4}$"

$\frac{3}{8}$" Cut two pieces from 320 sandpaper.

Trim corners.

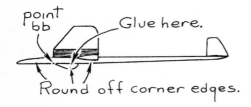

point
bb   Glue here.

Round off corner edges.

Fasten one piece to each side with Duco.

strip, with the grain as shown, and cut it out. Use thin, then regular glue to attach it to the body, placing the front edge at point *bb*. Hold it firmly against the body for about five minutes and wipe away the excess glue. When the glue dries, round off the corner edges between points *aa* and *cc* and also on the throwing grip. Finally, smooth off the whole body with your 400 block.

Cut two rectangular pieces ⅜ by ¾ inch from your 320 sandpaper sheet. Glue them to the body with Duco cement as shown. The rough sandpaper surface will give you an even firmer grip for throwing.

To lessen drag and improve performance, put a smooth finish on your glider. Dilute some sanding sealer with thinner, about three parts to one, in a small jar. Brush a coat of this mixture on the entire wing with your medium-size brush. Don't coat the rear edge of the finger grip. Next, brush a coat on the whole body, except for the sandpaper grips. When the sealer dries, smooth the wing and body lightly with your 400 block. Give the wings and body one more coat, and smooth them again. Don't use any sealer on the tail. Just give it a light final smoothing with the 400 block.

The final step in building is to check the wings for warps. Sight straight back from the nose toward the leading edge of the wing. Tilt the nose up slightly, and examine the shape of the two inner wing panels. Both sides should show the same shape, with their long sides, the leading and trailing edges, parallel. If the edges are not parallel and the panels are warped, steam the warps out. Boil some water in a kettle. Hold the warped part over the steaming spout. Be careful to keep your hands away from the steam. After a few moments, take the wing out of the steam and bend the warped edge the opposite way, as shown. Hold it there for a few moments to set the wood in its new position. Keep checking, steaming, and bending until both inner panels are straight across. Check the wing-tip panels too, and straighten them if they are warped. Adjust-

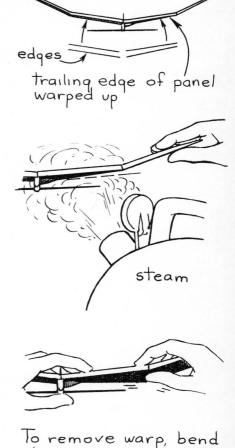

from the front

edges

trailing edge of panel warped up

steam

To remove warp, bend steamed panel the opposite way.

edges parallel — warp removed

ing a glider to fly properly requires some warping of the wings and tail. However, the only warps in the glider should be the ones you put there. To be sure that is the case, it is important to start out with flat, unwarped surfaces.

Your glider may fly surprisingly far at times, and you may lose it. Print your name, address, and telephone number on top of the wing. Then, anyone who finds the glider will be able to contact you, so you can get it back.

Congratulations! Your glider is finished.

3

Test Flying and Adjusting

After you finish building your glider, you have to adjust, or trim, it by making test flights. The ability to adjust a hand-launched glider properly is the mark of an expert flier. Many experts have learned the hard way by trial and error, using different adjustments over the years to find out what works and what doesn't. Although there is no substitute for real flying experience, if you follow the suggestions made in this chapter you can save yourself a lot of time and trouble learning how to adjust a glider.

A glider balances at a certain point along its length, where the forces of weight in front are equal to those in back. This balance point is called the center of gravity, or C.G. Gliders usually have the C.G. located from one half to two thirds back from the leading edge, along the width, or chord, of the wing. To fly properly, your glider should balance at 1¾ inches behind the leading edge, as shown on the

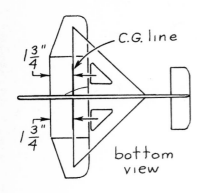

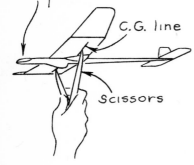

plan. Measure and mark 1¾ inches on both lower surfaces where the wings meet the body. Using your right triangle as shown, extend the marks outward on both inner panels.

Put some Plasticine clay on the nose. Have someone hold a pair of scissors with the tips up and open a few inches. Place one tip under each wing on the C.G. line. Add or remove clay until the glider balances level. Smooth the clay firmly around the top of the nose. Don't put any clay in front or on the bottom, since it may scrape off when the glider lands.

Test gliding is the first step in adjusting. It should be done on a fairly calm day with a wind of no more than five miles per hour. If you try to test in a strong breeze, you will not know if a poor glide is caused by improper adjustments or by wind gusts upsetting the glider. The best time to test fly is in the late afternoon or evening. Then lift from rising warm air currents generated by the sun's heat is less strong than in the morning or midday. Strong lift can carry a glider up and out of sight. So, in case you are fortunate enough to find the proper adjustments right at the start, fly late in the day to avoid losing your glider before you have a chance to use it. Always test fly over grass, never over concrete. Grass will usually cause little or no damage if something goes wrong. When you go out to test fly, take a box containing some clay, Duco cement, small balsa scraps, a razor blade, and the 320 sanding block.

Face the breeze to test glide. Raise the glider to eye level, so you can check the angle at which you release it. Point the nose down slightly, push the glider forward gently, and let it go. Don't release it with the nose up or it will stall. A stall occurs when the wing moves forward too slowly at too steep an angle. The wing suddenly loses lift, and the nose drops sharply. Suppose you release the glider properly, but the nose rises into a stall. Then add a little more clay to the nose until the glider moves forward level and gradually descends to the ground.

breeze

Point nose slightly down.

stall— Add a little clay.

steep, fast glide —
Bend up stabilizer trailing edge at center.
Remove a little clay.

If the glider descends quickly at a steep angle, bend up the unglued center portion of the stabilizer trailing edge slightly. Breathe on the balsa as you would to fog up a window. Bend it gently and gradually, so you don't split it. The slight steaming effect of your breath helps to warp the bent surface and set it in the new position. Use the same method when you warp the wing or the rudder. Test glide again. If the glider still descends steeply, wedge a thin piece of balsa between the stabilizer and the body to raise the unglued trailing edge a little more. Keep test gliding, removing a little clay at a time, until the glider just begins to stall. Then put a little clay back on.

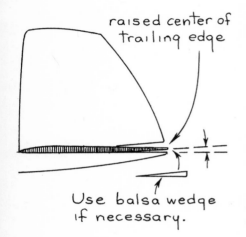

raised center of trailing edge

Use balsa wedge if necessary.

Now adjust the glide turn. After climbing high, a glider starts turning in circles as it drifts downwind. It is adjusted to turn this way for several reasons. For one thing, it stays over the flying field and in sight longer than it would if it flew straight downwind, which means shorter retrievals, fewer lost gliders, and longer flight times. This is especially necessary in windy weather, when models may drift away from the field quickly. Most important, its circling turn enables a glider to remain within warm, rising currents of air and so to make long, soaring flights.

The airfoil shape of the rudder provides some turning effect to begin with. In addition, it makes warping the rudder for more turn easy. The glider turns toward the opposite side from which it is thrown. Thus a right-handed flier uses left turn, a left-handed flier uses right turn. Looking at the rudder from the rear, warp it slightly at first, about one thirty-second of an inch to the left if you throw right-handed, about one thirty-second of an inch to the right if you throw left-handed.

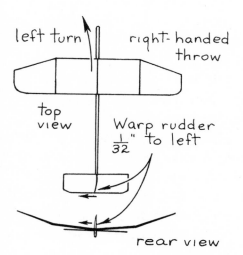

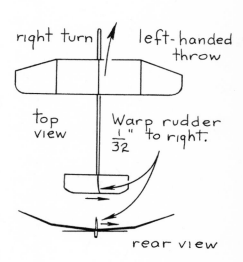

Test glide again. The glider should turn gradually along a curved path without either stalling or nosing down. If the glider stalls or dives, adjust the stabilizer and nose weight again until the glide is flat and smooth. If the glider keeps moving

breeze

Very little turn. Use more rudder warp. .

Proper turn. Glider banks gently.

Turns too tightly and banks steeply. Use less rudder warp.

straight, increase the rudder warp until the glide path starts to curve. If it follows a tight, sharp curve, decrease the rudder warp until the path turns gradually.

Suppose you have only warped the rudder slightly, but the glider banks very steeply into the turn. Stop and check the alignment of both sides of the wing. The inboard wing (on the inside of the turning circle) or the outboard wing (on the outside of the circle) may be warped. A warp with the leading edge up and the trailing edge down is called washin. Washout is the opposite, with the leading edge down and the trailing edge up.

Washin increases lift. Washin on the outboard wing may raise it enough to force the glider into a very tight turn, or even a spiral dive. Washout decreases lift. If the inboard wing has washout, it can force the glider to turn steeply or dive into the ground.

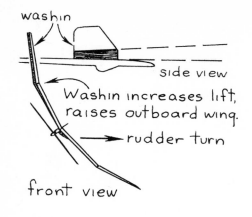

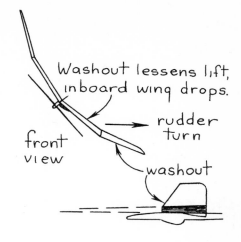

washin

side view

Washin increases lift, raises outboard wing.

→ rudder turn

front view

Washout lessens lift, inboard wing drops.

→ rudder turn

front view

washout

If you find washin on the outboard wing, washout on the inboard wing, or any other warps, remove them before you continue to fly. You may be able to do so at the flying field by simply twisting the wings the other way. If not, and if a car heater is available, hold the warped part in its flow of hot air and twist it straight. If the warp is very stubborn, stop flying, go home, and steam it out. Later check the wings now and then as you are flying to see that the warp you have removed has not returned.

Check the full glide pattern before you start throwing the glider high. To do so, bank the glider with the inboard wing down and throw it with moderate force right up into the glide turn. This low launch will require a little practice, because you must bank the glider opposite to the natural angle for throwing. Launch the glider several times to see if it glides the same way each time. An improper

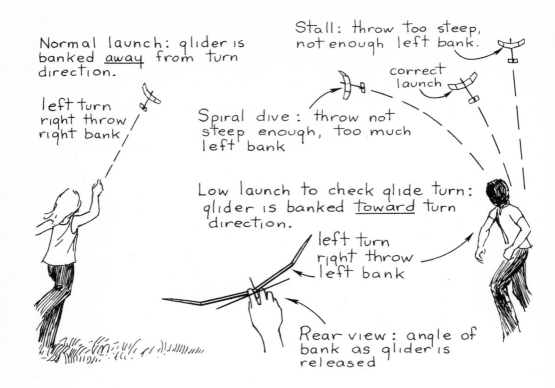

Normal launch: glider is banked _away_ from turn direction.

left turn
right throw
right bank

Stall: throw too steep, not enough left bank.

correct launch

Spiral dive: throw not steep enough, too much left bank

Low launch to check glide turn: glider is banked _toward_ turn direction.

left turn
right throw
left bank

Rear view: angle of bank as glider is released

launch will make it appear that the turn is poorly adjusted. If you throw too low or bank it too much, the angle of the launch alone may cause a spiral dive. If you throw too steeply with little or no bank, the glider will stall.

As the glider circles, check the turn adjustment. The turning circle should be about 50 to 100 feet wide. If the turn is too tight and the glider is banking sharply and threatening to spiral dive, try these adjustments. Take some warp out of the rudder, wedge the stabilizer trailing edge a little higher, and remove a little clay. Try changing these adjustments very slightly and one at a time, in the order given. Watch the effect as you continue low launching into the glide turn.

Another adjustment for controlling a tight turn is washin on the inboard wing. This creates more lift on the inboard side, holds the glider up, and widens the turning circle. To put in washin, twist the entire wing by raising the leading edge until you can see about one sixteenth of an inch of the trailing edge below the tip break.

If the glider heads straight instead of circling, or if it circles too widely, increase the rudder warp. A helpful adjustment to avoid the danger of spiral diving when you have to tighten the turn is to increase the tilt of the stabilizer. Stabilizer tilt, or stab tilt, as modelers call it, boosts the turning effect of the rudder. The glider turns toward the raised end of the stab in flat, tight circles. Stab tilt is primarily a glide turn adjustment. It has only a slight effect on the climb, so it is safer to use than extra rudder warp. The stab on your glider already has some built-in tilt.

To adjust the stab tilt, sight straight back from the nose and check the alignment of the inboard wing and the stab. To increase the tilt, raise the inboard end of the stab about one sixteenth of an inch by twisting the rear part of the body. Don't twist in too much tilt. Try to use no more

To control tight turn, warp inboard wing, trailing edge down.

front view

turn direction

Washin creates more lift to hold wing up.

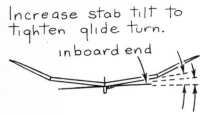

Increase stab tilt to tighten glide turn.

inboard end

Limit stab tilt to one-half the dihedral angle.

than half the dihedral angle of the wing. The springy body wood will tend to twist back to its former position, so when you get home set the tilt so that it will not change. Dissolve the stab glue joint with thinner, tilt the stab, and reglue it.

If you find that your glider is circling too tightly but not banking steeply, it probably has too much stab tilt. A tighter turn than necessary cuts down gliding efficiency and lowers the flight time. To open up the flat turn, decrease the tilt by lowering the inboard end of the stab.

Although stab tilt tends to give a fairly flat turn, the necessary amount of rudder warp plus the tilt may cause a steep banking circle. A good way to keep the turn flat is to add more washin to the inboard wing. Gradually balance the adjustments—rudder turn and stab tilt against wing washin—until the glider circles properly. Remember that a tight turn requires more washin, a wide turn requires less.

Once the glide turn is adjusted, start using a full throw. Fly on the largest field you can find. Again pick a fairly calm day. Launch from the upwind side of the field, the side from which the wind is blowing, so your glider has plenty of room to drift downwind without hitting anything. Face the wind to launch.

Your throw must combine the angle of bank—the tilt of the glider sideways—with

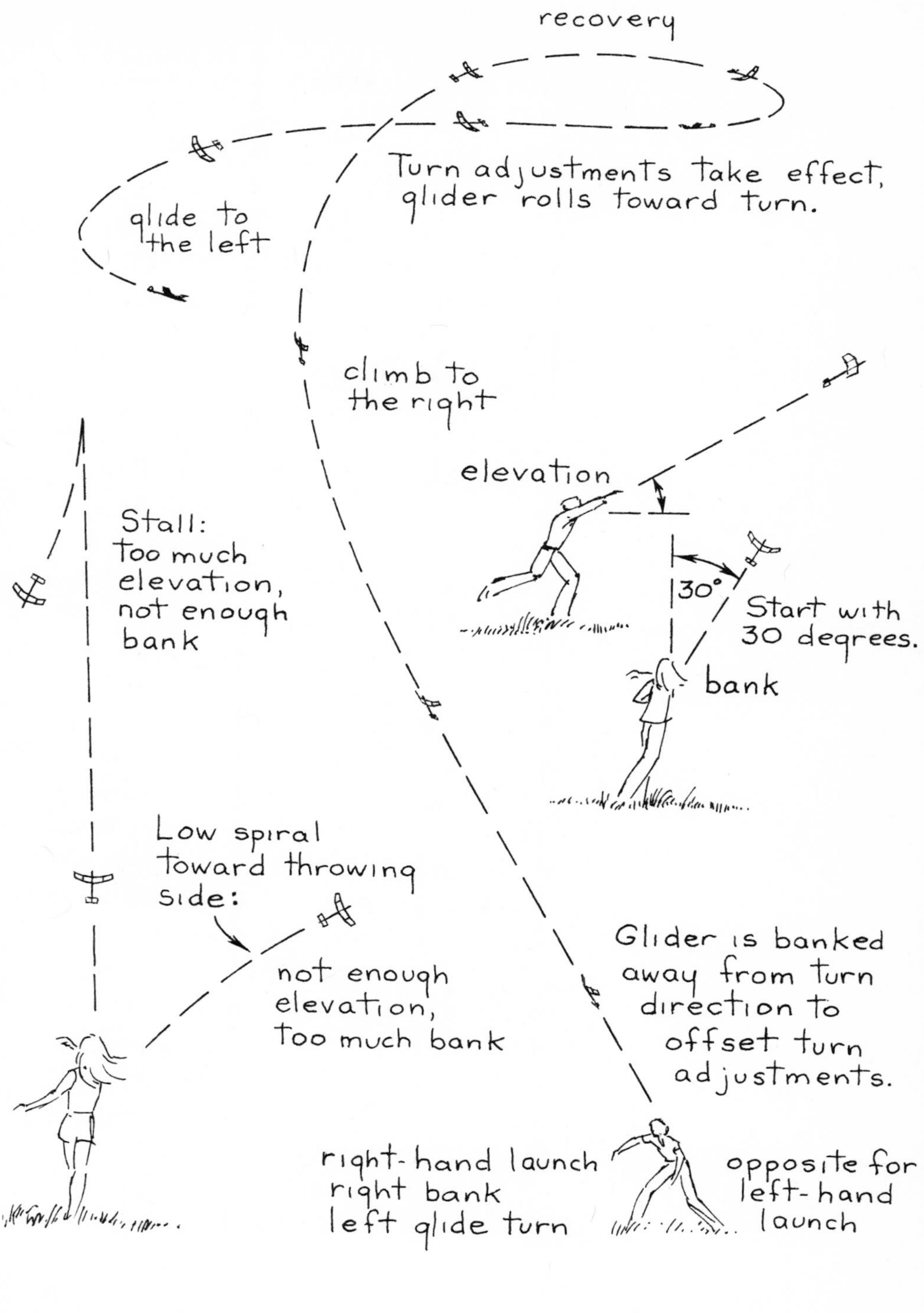

recovery

Turn adjustments take effect, glider rolls toward turn.

glide to the left

climb to the right

elevation

Stall: Too much elevation, not enough bank

30° Start with 30 degrees.

bank

Low spiral toward throwing side:

not enough elevation, too much bank

Glider is banked away from turn direction to offset turn adjustments.

right-hand launch right bank left glide turn

opposite for left-hand launch

the angle of elevation—how high you point the nose. Bank the glider to the side opposite its turn to help offset the turn adjustments as it climbs. Toward the top of the climb, as the banking effect diminishes, the launch power is used up and the glider slows down. The turn adjustments take over, causing the glider to roll into the glide turn. This point, called roll-out, recovery, or transition, is a crucial part of the flight.

Bank the glider about 30 degrees to start. Too little bank will cause it to stall at the top of the climb. Too much bank will cause it to spiral low off toward your throwing side. Don't use a full sidearm throw. It is hard to control, and an excess of bank can cause a zooming spiral dive into the ground. The angle of elevation—how steep you throw—is as important as how much you bank the glider. Throwing too steeply will cause it to stall at the top, because the glider reaches its peak with its nose too high and with insufficient airspeed. Remember that a steeper launch requires more power to carry the glider smoothly over its peak into the glide turn without stalling. If you find that your glider keeps stalling at the top of its climb, increase the angle of bank and decrease the angle of elevation.

You are launching properly, but your glider is not climbing as it should. What is wrong? First of all, small improper adjustments may not show up at the relatively slow speeds of test gliding. However, at high-launching speeds of up to seventy-five miles per hour or more, a wing, stab, or rudder bent even slightly the wrong way can suddenly cause a lot of trouble. This greater sensitivity at high speed means that you have to adjust the climb as well as the glide.

Suppose your glider heads up steeply, stalls, and plunges straight down. It does so because the wing and stab are set at exactly the same angle to the body. This setting is the secret behind getting the glider to climb high. However, in order to recover well at the top of the climb, there must be at least a small difference in the angle to the body between the wing and the stab. The stab must be set at a slightly lower angle to the body than the wing, at what is called negative incidence. This difference, however, must not come from the original gluing but from the adjustments you bend in later.

One way to provide negative incidence is to tilt the entire stab down in front at a lower angle to the body than the wing's. However, during the high-speed launching phase of the flight, this adjustment usually causes the glider to reach its peak too soon and reduces the height of the climb. With too much negative incidence the glider

no negative incidence

wing and stab set at same angle to body

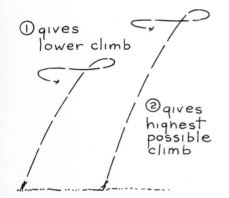

wing   stab

① negative incidence by tilting entire stab

② negative incidence by bending up center of stab trailing edge

① gives lower climb

② gives highest possible climb

may even loop on launching the way inexpensive ready-made gliders often do. There is a better way to achieve a high climb yet still have enough negative incidence for a good recovery. The stab, set at exactly the same angle to the body as the wing, should be bent up slightly in the center at the trailing edge. Always try to use as little negative incidence as possible.

A safe method of adjusting the stab incidence is to bend up the center trailing edge an extra amount to start with by pushing in the balsa wedge. At first the glider may even loop. That is safer, however, than a vertical dive from high in the air. It is simpler to correct a looping climb than it is to glue some shattered pieces of wood together. As you continue to launch, gradually bend down the trailing edge slightly by pulling the wedge out farther or removing it. You will see the height of the climb increase until there comes a point at which the glider starts to recover poorly. Then bend up the stab trailing edge very slightly, and you will have the best adjustment.

If your glider persists in diving or looping despite these adjustments, use the straight edge of your ruler to check the wing-stab setting. Diving is probably due to the stab being glued on at a higher, positive, angle than that of the wing. Looping is probably caused by the stab being set at

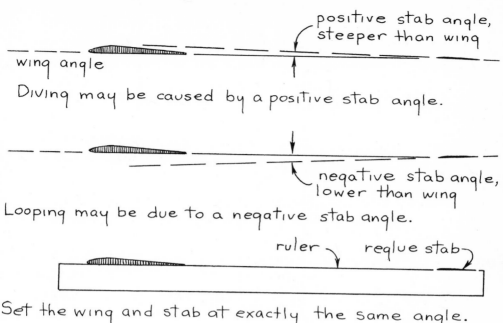

Diving may be caused by a positive stab angle.

Looping may be due to a negative stab angle.

Set the wing and stab at exactly the same angle.

a lower, negative, angle than that of the wing. If the wing-stab setting is not precisely the same, dissolve the stab glue joint with thinner and reglue the stab to the body so that it is at exactly the same angle as the wing.

Another problem you may have in adjusting the climb is controlling how much the glider rolls. There are two possible extremes. The glider may roll sharply toward the turn direction on launch, even though you give it plenty of bank. The recovery is prompt, and the glide turn works perfectly, but the tight spiral climb is using up too much power that could be used to gain more altitude if you could straighten it out. Or the glider may climb too readily toward your throwing side and reach only a low altitude far off to the side. Although the glide turn works well, the glider does not roll enough, resists recovering smoothly, and requires very precise launching.

An effective way to control the climb roll is to use stab twist. Since the stab surface area is small and close to the body, it exerts less leverage on the body than the wing area. Thus stab twist affects flight mostly at the higher speed achieved right after launching. As the speed decreases toward the top of the climb, the twist has less effect. Finally, at the slow glide speed, it has only a slight effect on the turn. Stab twist is a valuable adjustment for controlling the climb because it has a strong effect only at high speed.

The stab trailing edge is twisted up on one side and down on the other. The raised side has washout and so less lift, the lowered side has washin and so more lift. This adjustment creates a rolling force. Depending upon which way the stab is twisted, the degree of climb roll can be increased or decreased.

Suppose your glider glides well but climbs in a tight, rolling spiral toward the turn direction, even though you give it plenty of bank. Warp the outboard trailing edge of the stab up slightly and the in-board trailing edge down slightly. The warp will cause a rolling force against the climb roll and straighten out the climb. Since this adjustment acts against the rudder turn during the climb, it allows you to warp the rudder a good deal for a fairly tight turn without the danger of spiral diving on the climb. In addition, the

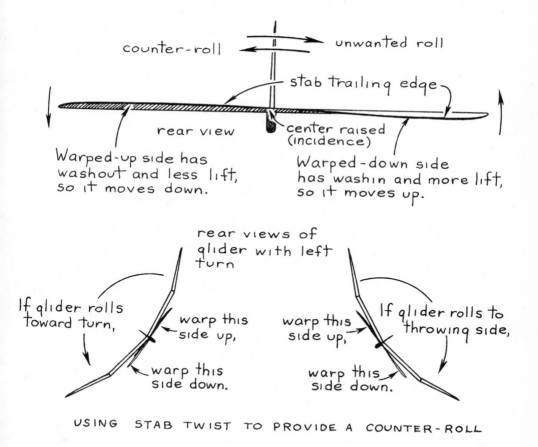

USING STAB TWIST TO PROVIDE A COUNTER-ROLL

extra amount of rudder warp also helps the glider to roll out very promptly.

If your glider goes to the other extreme and climbs too readily off toward your throwing side, twist the stab the other way. Warp the outboard trailing edge down and the inboard trailing edge up. This adjustment will increase the climb roll and smooth the recovery. When you use stab twist, it may or may not be necessary to warp both sides. Sometimes you can create enough rolling force by warping one side only and leaving the other side alone. Experiment to see what works best for you.

Your glider is climbing high and gliding in smooth, flat circles. You have achieved your goal of successfully flying a hand-launched glider. At first you may think that there is nothing more to it. But flying is really an endless process of adapting to changing conditions of wind and weather. As conditions change, you have to make changes in the adjustments as well as in your technique of launching. In order to make longer flights, you have to find and use rising air currents, or lift. Adjusting is really just the beginning.

4

Flying Your Glider

A good flight starts with a good throw. Even with an excellent, carefully adjusted glider, a poor throw produces a poor flight. Since the flight performance of your glider depends so much on your performance in throwing, keep checking yourself as you fly. How well are you launching, and how could you do it better?

You may have been throwing almost flat-footedly, or by taking only one or two steps forward. When athletes throw the javelin, or throw to home plate from the outfield, they run forward to add momentum to the force of their throw. A running throw is more powerful. It also sets up a rhythm that becomes automatic, increasing control. With greater power and better control, you can throw your glider higher more consistently, so you should use a running throw for launching.

The idea is to gain speed with running steps, then to make a final spring forward from the foot on your throwing side as you

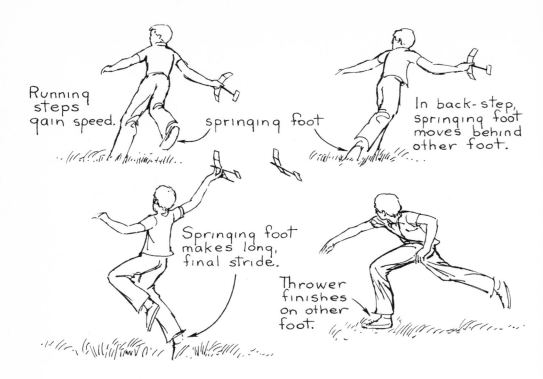

Running steps gain speed.

springing foot

In back-step, springing foot moves behind other foot.

Springing foot makes long, final stride.

Thrower finishes on other foot.

release the glider. The fullest development of this natural running throw, sometimes called the backstep, is used by many top fliers to gain maximum power. The preparatory step just before release places your springing foot behind the other foot, which allows you to take a longer final springing stride. Always start running with the same foot and take the same number of steps. This way you will develop a consistent rhythm that will enable you to launch the glider with the same elevation, bank, and speed each time. Above all, don't forget that control is much more important than sheer force.

Improving your throw will help your glider to stay up longer. An even better way to get longer flights, however, is to take advantage of rising air currents, or lift. Lift is not to be found just anywhere or anytime you might be ready to fly. You have to look for it in certain places and often to wait for it to develop. Thus, knowing when and where to throw your glider can be just as important as knowing how to throw it.

How does lift affect the glide? A good hand-launched glider, descending at normal sinking speed, loses about two feet of altitude each second. Lift slows its sinking speed, causing the glider to stay up longer. In air rising at one foot per second, the glider will sink at two minus one, or one foot per second. Thus, a glider that would normally stay up thirty to forty seconds might fly for sixty to eighty seconds.

Sometimes a glider will circle without gaining or losing altitude. Then you can be sure it is soaring in lift rising at about two feet per second, equal to its sinking speed. If the glider encounters lift that is rising strongly, say at eight feet per second, it will soar and gain altitude at eight minus two, or six feet per second. At such times the glider seems to have suddenly flown onto an express elevator climbing toward the top of the sky. In booming lift of twelve feet or more per second, a glider

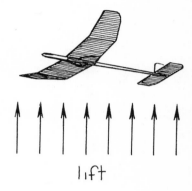

lift

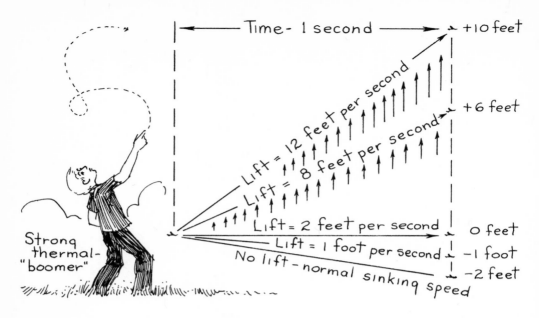

Time - 1 second → +10 feet

Lift = 12 feet per second

Lift = 8 feet per second → +6 feet

Lift = 2 feet per second · 0 feet

Lift = 1 foot per second · −1 foot

No lift - normal sinking speed · −2 feet

Strong thermal- "boomer"

HOW LIFT AFFECTS THE GLIDE

will rise ten feet or more each second, gaining over six hundred feet in one minute. Such an ascent doesn't happen often, but it certainly may, and the glider shrinks quickly to a tiny circling speck.

Thermals provide the strongest lift for soaring. When the sun heats an area, some parts heat up more rapidly than others, and the air above them becomes hotter. Paved areas, dirt roads, and dry fields heat up faster and give off more heat than woods, wet grass, and green crops. The air above a heated place rises and draws air from surrounding cooler places. This air is heated and rises in turn. The rising air expands upward in a large bubble. Sur-

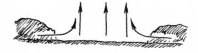
Air above heated area rises.

Heat bubble expands.

Bubble curls up and spills over.

Bubble rises, fed by column of heated air.

cool air

Bubble separates from ground and rises.

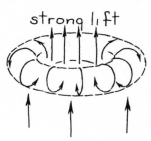
strong lift

Bubble forms thermal shell.

rounding air flows into the bubble and enlarges it so that it curls up and spills over. Finally, cooler air around the bubble flows in beneath it, and it starts to rise.

Depending upon how fast it rises and upon wind speed, the bubble may continue to be fed by a column of air rising from the ground. On calm days, minutes may pass before the bubble finally separates from the feeding column. On windy days, thermals break off swiftly and sharply. The rising bubble develops into a thermal shell as warm air flowing up through the center and spilling out over the top forms a doughnut-shaped ring of circulating air. Gliders soar by circling within the strong lift at the center as the thermal shell rises and drifts downwind.

The best way to get a long flight is to throw your glider up into a rising thermal shell. But how do you find thermals? Pick a sunny day with light winds to start practicing. It is easiest to find thermals under such conditions. If possible, stand downwind from a paved area. Face toward the breeze. Get the feel of the speed and temperature of the air blowing across your face and hands. Notice how the air calms down every so often and becomes warmer.

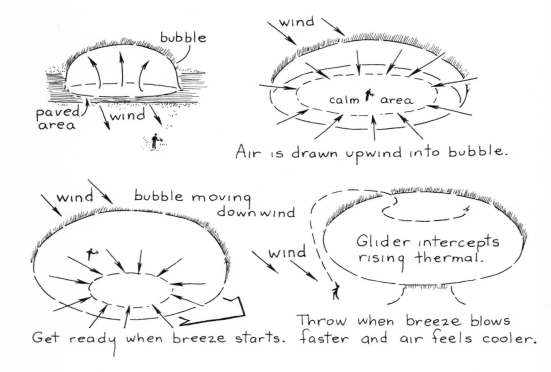

Air is drawn upwind into bubble.

Get ready when breeze starts. Throw when breeze blows faster and air feels cooler.

When it does, you are standing within an expanding bubble of heated air.

The bubble draws in air from all around it. Air drawn back upwind cancels out the effect of the wind itself for a moment and produces the calm. You can feel the heat building up all around. This is a sign to get ready. As the bubble moves slowly downwind across the field, the breeze starts blowing again, lightly at first, from its former direction. The bubble is starting to move away, drawing the air with it. Don't throw yet.

Throw your glider just when the breeze starts blowing harder and the air feels cooler. The sudden faster flow is caused by the surrounding air feeding downwind into the bubble, added to the resumed normal flow of the wind as the bubble moves away. Launched against the direction of the wind, your glider climbs in a spiral slanting downwind, intercepts the thermal, and starts to circle within its center.

Many serious fliers use thermal indicators to find lift. Of the various types, streamers are the best for hand-launch flying. The simplest streamer is the wind stick, a quarter-inch dowel, three feet long, sharpened on one end and stuck into the ground. A one-inch wide streamer of plastic food wrap, about two feet long, is taped to the top of the stick. Placed upwind, the

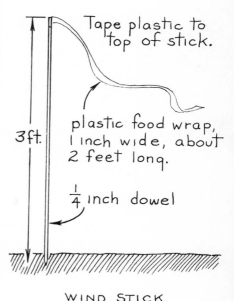

Tape plastic to top of stick.

3 ft.

plastic food wrap, 1 inch wide, about 2 feet long.

$\frac{1}{4}$ inch dowel

WIND STICK

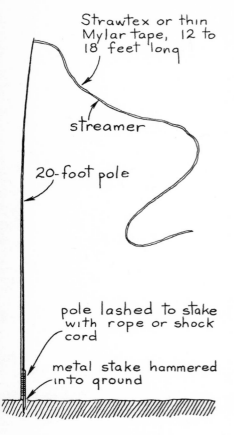

Strawtex or thin Mylar tape, 12 to 18 feet long

streamer

20-foot pole

pole lashed to stake with rope or shock cord

metal stake hammered into ground

THERMAL STREAMER

streamer shows you the wind speed and direction. You can see in advance when the approaching air is calming down or speeding up. If a strong thermal bubble is building off to one side, the streamer will point that way.

A more accurate and sensitive indicator uses an extra lightweight streamer atop a twenty-foot pole. A telescoping Fiberglas fishing pole is best. A pointed stake of angle iron or heavy aluminum is hammered into the ground, and the pole is lashed to it with rope or elastic shock cord. The streamer is made from Strawtex, a material used in artificial flowers, or from thin Mylar tape.

At twenty feet up, the streamer is above most ground turbulence, so it gives a clearer picture of passing thermals than the wind stick. In lighter winds and strong lift, the streamer will actually point up-

Streamer blows steadily in normal wind.

Streamer drops as calm, warmer area passes.

Streamer points upward as thermal bubble expands.

Streamer lowers and blows steadily again.

launch

ward as the bubble expands. Then, when air fills in behind the bubble, the streamer lowers and starts blowing downwind. That is the time to launch. In stronger winds, thermals pass more rapidly, so the streamer's indication is more momentary. Frequent practice in all kinds of winds and weather is the best way to get the most from any thermal detector, including the feel of the air on your own body.

Lift can also be present without thermals on calm, damp, overcast days and in early-morning or late-evening dew. Moisture evaporating from warm fields and rising into cooler air above can provide surprisingly buoyant flying conditions. At such times, paved areas are usually cooler and drier, so the lift above them is weaker. This effect is just the opposite of sunny days, when strong lift rises from paved areas. So to get longer flights when there are no thermal conditions, try flying over grassy places.

The best adjustments for calmer air and large, slowly developing thermals are different from those used for wind and small, brisk thermals. To fly best in calmer air, widen the glide turn by using a bit less rudder warp and stab tilt. By turning in larger circles, your glider can cover a broader area and seek out calm-air thermals that are often difficult to find and intercept as you launch. If the glider enters

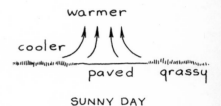

SUNNY DAY

OVERCAST, EARLY MORNING, LATE EVENING

a thermal, the turn will tighten up due to an increase in airspeed. Even without thermals, a wide turn lowers the glider's sinking speed to a minimum and increases flight time. As you widen the turn, you will probably need a little less washin on the inboard wing.

There is another important combination of adjustments to use for improving calm-air performance. First, shift the C.G. a little farther back by removing a bit of nose weight. Then decrease the negative incidence in the stab by bending down the trailing edge slightly. This will allow the glider to climb higher in calm air before it peaks at the top. It also permits trimming the wing's gliding angle very close to a stall, thus increasing its glide performance. However, be sure not to overdo the adjustment or the glider will not recover at the top of the climb.

Strong thermals and windy, turbulent conditions call for just the opposite of calm-air adjustments. On a windy day with strong lift, thermals are smaller and break away faster. To circle and stay within small, strong thermals, your glider should have more turn than it does for calmer air. Without enough turn, the glider may not intercept a thermal successfully and may fly right through it or bounce off one side. Even if it does enter the thermal, it may stall or be thrown out. A

	calm day, large, slow-moving thermals	windy day, small, fast-moving thermals
turn	wide	tight
nose weight	less	more
stab incidence	less	more
wing washin	less	more

little extra stab tilt or rudder warp or both will tighten the turn and will usually require more washin to hold up the inboard wing.

There is also a combination adjustment for better flying in strong thermals and windy weather. Shift the C.G. a little farther forward by adding some nose weight. Then increase the negative incidence by bending up the center of the stab trailing edge a little. In turbulent air the airflow strikes the wing at constantly changing angles. The forward C.G. and increased negative incidence in the stab give greater front-to-rear stability in this shifting airflow to prevent stalling or diving.

Don't think of calm-air and turbulent-air adjustments as extreme opposites. The actual changes in C.G. location and in wing and tail warp may be slight. Nevertheless, they are important to keep in mind as two different ways to adjust. Some expert fliers solve the problem of changing adjustments by using two gliders: one trimmed for calmer air, the other for windy weather. As you continue to build and fly, you may want to do this too. Flying differently trimmed gliders allows you to concentrate on finding lift without bothering to think about changing adjustments.

One thing you do have to think about when you fly in windy weather is launching properly. First of all, you will probably find that you don't have to throw as hard. The wind creates a much faster airflow into which you launch your glider and supplies a lot of lift for a very strong starting boost. If you throw hard, you may find that your climb pattern gets out of control. In wind it is best to concentrate on how and when to throw, not how hard.

If there are thermals present, the best indication you may get is a brief moment when the wind slows down. Don't depend upon finding a calm, warm period. Windy-weather thermals are usually too small and fast moving to cancel out the downwind airflow. When you are ready to fly, wait and watch for a while to see how frequently the calmer periods occur. Place your wind stick or streamer pole farther upwind than you would on a day with light

Streamer blows level and steadily in wind.

Streamer momentarily slacks off as thermal passes.

launch

winds. This will give you more time to react to the approaching air before it reaches you. Launch just at the moment when the streamer slacks off.

In windy conditions, the glider should be trimmed with an adequate amount of turn. You need enough turn to swing the glider around into the wind again and steadily gain altitude after the initial downwind turn due to your launching bank. With insufficient climb turn, the glider may keep heading downwind, gain less altitude, and miss the thermal you were aiming for. On the other hand, without enough turn and roll in the climb, your glider may loop if you launch directly into the wind, due to excess lift in the strong airflow. A glider that climbs tightly has greater resistance to being thrown off its path by wind gusts. The smaller climbing circle allows it to intercept compact, fast-moving thermals on the way up.

The interaction of wind direction and launch direction can cause problems. The glider reaches its peak and recovers heading at an angle to the wind that depends on how much your glider turns during the climb as well as on the direction you throw it. The timing of launching to catch small thermals in wind is often very critical. If the glider heads off straight downwind at the peak, it may speed out ahead of the thermal. On the other hand, if it

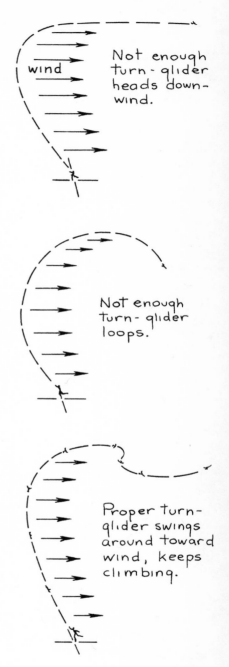

Not enough turn - glider heads down-wind.

Not enough turn - glider loops.

Proper turn-glider swings around toward wind, keeps climbing.

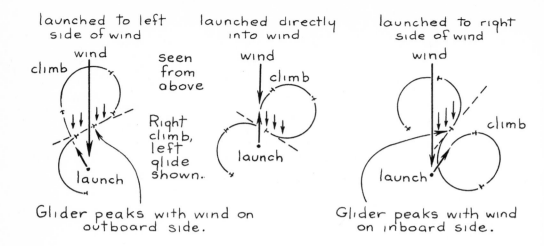

launched to left side of wind

launched directly into wind

launched to right side of wind

seen from above

Right climb, left glide shown.

Glider peaks with wind on outboard side.

Glider peaks with wind on inboard side.

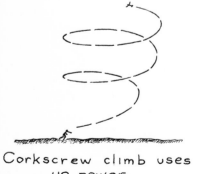

Corkscrew climb uses up power.

heads straight into the wind, it will hesitate before turning, possibly stall, and fall behind the thermal.

The glider should peak with the wind blowing on one side or the other. If it blows on the outboard side, it can lift that wing and help to tilt the glider smoothly into its glide turn. Yet some fliers like to peak with the inboard side toward the wind. Other fliers use a very tight spiral climb and do not worry about which way the glider is heading at the top. Tight spiraling uses up a lot of power and lessens the height of the climb, however. When thermals are weak at lower levels but stronger higher up, this can be a real disadvantage. So try to avoid a corkscrew climb.

When you practice in wind, use a wind stick to check the wind direction and your

launch direction. Try launching at different angles to the left and right, as well as
directly into the wind. Try different degrees of bank and elevation. Watch your
glider as it reaches the peak to see how well
it recovers and starts circling. If you have
a friend flying with you, ask him to stand
off at a distance where he can watch the
glider better than you can from directly
below.

Practicing in windy weather or when
thermals are weak may not seem to make
much sense. However, you cannot always
find good weather on the days when you
are ready to fly. Learning how to take best
advantage of unfavorable conditions is a
challenge in itself. Many fliers can do well
with light winds and strong thermals. But
few can really fly well when the weather
gets rough and thermals are hard to find.

5

Contest Flying

As you continue to build and fly hand-launched gliders, you may want to compete in contests to try your skill against that of other fliers. Striving to win stimulates you to build your gliders more carefully, adjust them to their top performance, and make every throw count.

The Academy of Model Aeronautics, or A.M.A., is the national organization that controls contest activities in the United States. Contests are sponsored and conducted by clubs chartered by the A.M.A. Hand-launched gliders are an officially designated class of free-flight models, and most free-flight contests include an event for them. Trophies, merchandise, or gift certificates are awarded to the first-, second-, and third-place winners. To fly in an A.M.A. contest, you must be a licensed A.M.A. member. Membership age categories are Junior, under fifteen years old; Senior, fifteen to nineteen years old; and Open, nineteen years and over. Most con-

tests have separate awards for Juniors or
for Juniors and Seniors combined. Information about joining the A.M.A. and
N.F.F.S., the National Free Flight Society,
is listed in the back of this book.

The A.M.A. contest rules for hand-
launched gliders allow a total of six flights,
with each flight limited to a maximum, or
max, of two minutes. From the six flights,
the three longest flight times are added
together to give the flier's score. If the flier
should make three maxes, giving him a
total of six minutes, he is then allowed to
make fly-off flights of two minutes until
he fails to get a max. Fly-off flights are used
to break tie scores in case two or more fliers
"max out" with three two-minute flights.

Another type of contest uses the German
rules. This system calls for a total of the
best six out of ten flights, with a one-
minute max time. Three- or four-man
teams fly together for a total team score.
The German rules place greater emphasis
on consistent performance. In addition, the
one-minute max permits using smaller

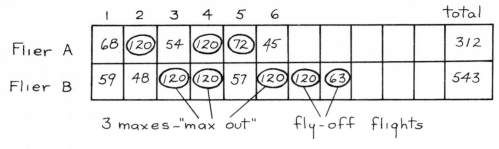

	1	2	3	4	5	6					total
Flier A	68	(120)	54	(120)	(72)	45					312
Flier B	59	48	(120)	(120)	57	(120)	(120)	(63)			543

3 maxes – "max out" fly-off flights

A.M.A. RULES SCORES

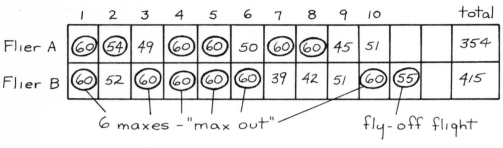

	1	2	3	4	5	6	7	8	9	10		total
Flier A	(60)	(54)	49	(60)	(60)	50	(60)	(60)	45	51		354
Flier B	(60)	52	(60)	(60)	(60)	(60)	39	42	51	(60)	(55)	415

6 maxes – "max out" fly-off flight

GERMAN RULES SCORES

flying fields, a very important point in built-up areas where open land is hard to find.

There are international postal contests for hand-launched gliders in which teams of fliers from all around the world compete. They are called postals because the teams fly at their local fields on any day during a given month and mail their scores to the club sponsoring the contest. The teams are then notified about the results. International postals use the German rules. Postals are also conducted by American clubs for individual fliers using the A.M.A. rules. Some of these contests are limited to Junior fliers. In a recent postal contest sponsored by the Sky-Scrapers, an event was added for the longest single flight, with the timers permitted to use binoculars to keep the glider in sight as long as possible. This event was won with a flight of over fifteen minutes, and second place was won by a fourteen-minute-plus flight.

POSTAL CONTEST EMBLEM

Contest flying requires a high-climbing glider that can soar on moderate lift. The fastest and easiest way to improve a glider's glide is to lighten its weight. However, if you lighten a glider too much, you cannot throw it as high. In general, the smaller and heavier the glider is, the higher you can throw it, but the faster it will sink in the glide. Conversely, the larger and lighter the glider the better it will glide, but the less altitude you will be able to reach with it. So the best weight for any glider is a compromise: heavy enough to climb well, light enough to glide well.

Since you probably didn't use light wood for the wings and tail of your first glider, it could be heavier than it should be. You can check the weight approximately on a small postal scale that measures down to a quarter ounce. Your glider should weigh from ½ to ⅝ ounce, including the nose clay. If it weighs more, lighten it to improve its glide performance. Since

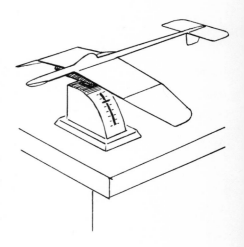

the wing accounts for more than half the total weight, start taking off weight there.

Remove weight by sanding a concave curvature into the flat bottom surface of the wing. Undercamber, as this curvature is called, both lightens the wing and gives it a more efficient airfoil shape to improve the glide. Start sanding the undercamber with a piece of 240 sandpaper, not the block. Sand only the inner portion of the bottom surface, not the leading or trailing edges. As you get closer to the final curvature, switch to a piece of 320 sandpaper and sand lengthwise along the grain to prevent cutting the wood fibers. Finally, smooth the undercambered surface with a piece of 400 sandpaper.

As you work, hold the wing up toward the light to check the depth and smoothness of the undercamber along the length of the wing with a straight edge as shown. The undercamber should be the same out past the tip breaks. The depth should be from one thirty-second of an inch to a *scant* one sixteenth of an inch. Too much curvature will cause too much drag and hold back the climb, and it may also thin the wing so much that it lacks strength to resist hard throwing. Be sure not to let the undercamber get deeper than a *scant* one sixteenth of an inch. Flatten the undercamber toward the tips to lessen the drag there.

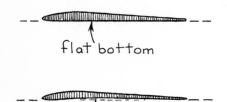

flat bottom

undercamber

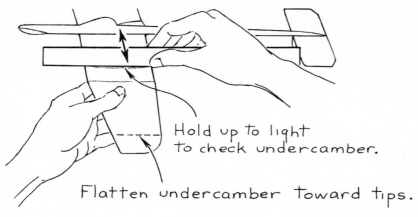

Hold up to light to check undercamber.

Flatten undercamber toward tips.

maximum undercamber $\frac{1}{32}$ inch to scant $\frac{1}{16}$ inch

Do not sand leading or trailing edges.

It is also possible to get a fine glide with a flat-bottom airfoil shape, so long as the glider is light enough. However, to build a light flat-bottom wing you must use light wood, preferably in the five-pound range. A light flat-bottom wing has extra stiffness and strength for launching. Without undercamber, the glider can climb faster and higher. Thus most fliers prefer flat-bottom wings if they do not need to cut down on weight.

You can see that as you continue to build, it is important to obtain better, lighter wood. The best way to get good wood is to order directly from a balsa supplier by mail. "Contest grade" balsa runs from four to six pounds. You can order the weight and grain in the sizes you want and save yourself the trouble of searching through hobby stores. A source for contest balsa is listed in the back of this book.

Eventually you will probably want to get a scale that measures fractions of grams or ounces accurately. A photographic materials balance is a good scale for this purpose. You can weigh the wood when you receive your order, grade it exactly, and have it ready for building. Tables are available listing the various sheet sizes of balsa and their weight in grams or ounces for different weight grades. By checking the sheet size against the actual weight, you can find the exact weight grade of each sheet, such as 5.2 or 5.8 pounds, and mark the sheet for future use. An accurate scale will also help you to keep track of the weight of different parts as you build, to insure that the glider's total weight is satisfactory.

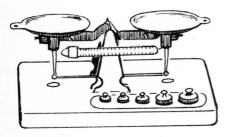

Saving weight in general is a good idea, but saving it on particular parts of the glider is even better. The tail and wing tips should be kept as light as possible. Since these parts are farthest from the C.G., their weight exerts considerable leverage. Under balanced conditions, a heavy tail and heavy wing tips are no problem. However, when the glider's flight balance is upset by a poor launch recovery or a sudden wind gust, the heavy tail or wing tips start moving.

Their moving weight creates inertia, which tends to keep them moving. This hinders the glider's return to equilibrium. For example, in a stall the glider's nose swings up and the tail drops. A heavy tail causes a lot of inertia and slows the glider's return to level flight. A light tail causes little inertia, and the glider can regain balance rapidly. The same is true of inertia caused by the wing tips when the glider's side-to-side balance is upset and it banks steeply.

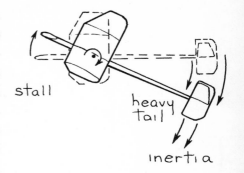

The lighter you can make the tail and wing tips, while still keeping them strong enough, the easier your gliders will be to adjust and the more stable they will be in flight. In addition, lightening the tail allows you to remove some of the nose weight required to balance it. This decreases the total weight of the glider. Such factors are important in contest flying.

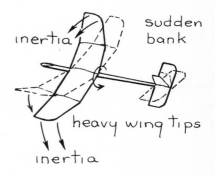

You can lighten the tail by thinning the stabilizer and rudder. Always thin them by tapering from the body out to the tips, as shown. Be careful here, because very thin sections flex too much at high launching speed, causing extra drag and possible breakage. However, by using a 1/16-inch thickness in lightweight C-grain, you can keep the tail surfaces rigid enough and still reduce their weight. Once your glider is adjusted, you can thin the rear of the body somewhat and round it off a bit more to lighten the tail. Some fliers use four- to

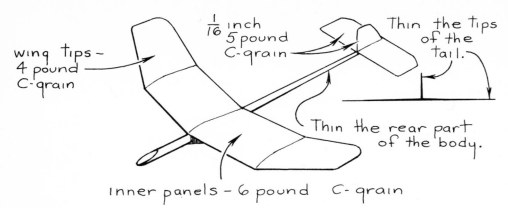

wing tips – 4 pound C-grain

$\frac{1}{16}$ inch 5 pound C-grain

Thin the tips of the tail.

Thin the rear part of the body.

Inner panels – 6 pound C-grain

MAKING THE TAIL AND WING TIPS LIGHTER

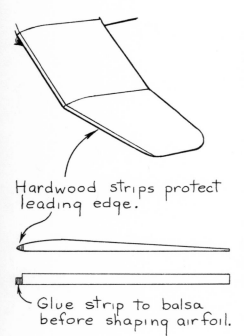

Hardwood strips protect leading edge.

Glue strip to balsa before shaping airfoil.

five-pound wood in the wing tips, to keep them as light as possible, with heavier wood in the center panels for extra strength where launching stresses are the greatest.

When you use lightweight wood in the wing, add spruce or basswood strips along the leading edge for protection. Most contest fliers use spruce, basswood, or pine for glider bodies. Hardwood can withstand more shock than balsa if the glider dives from high up. However, you have to be careful to keep the tail of a hardwood body light enough.

A very smooth finish keeps surface drag to a minimum. As long as it does not add too much weight, a fine finish is helpful, especially during the high-speed climb. You can use two coats of sanding sealer, smoothing between coats with 400 paper, then add a few coats of clear dope mixed with some thinner, sanding with 500 finishing paper between coats. Avoid doping the rear portion of the stab and rudder. Dope warps thin surfaces and makes them brittle, so they may crack when you try to adjust them. Many fliers do not put any finish on the tail, relying instead on a final sanding with 500 paper to give a high degree of smoothness. The raw balsa tail is lighter, and its greater flexibility makes it last longer. With experience you can decide what kind of finish you want to use.

As your flying improves, a new problem arises. After you find a thermal and send your glider soaring skyward, how do you keep from losing it? How do you bring it down before it flies out of sight? To make thermal flights of contest duration, as well as to practice on small fields where long flights are impossible, you have to use a dethermalizer.

A dethermalizer interrupts the glide after a certain period of time and causes the glider to descend rapidly. There are a number of different kinds, but they all use the same method of timing. The flight time depends upon a short length of cotton rope that burns steadily at about a quarter-inch per minute and acts as the timing fuse. Depending upon the length of fuse, the flight can be timed for anywhere from a few seconds to two minutes. The fuse rope burns through a small rubber band looped over it. The release

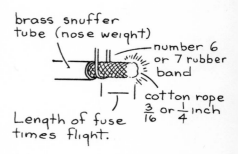

brass snuffer tube (nose weight)
number 6 or 7 rubber band
cotton rope $\frac{3}{16}$ or $\frac{1}{4}$ inch
Length of fuse times flight.

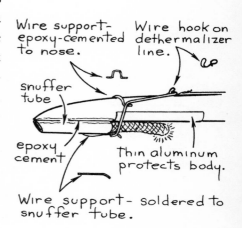

Wire support- epoxy-cemented to nose.
Wire hook on dethermalizer line.
snuffer tube
epoxy cement
thin aluminum protects body.
Wire support- soldered to snuffer tube.

of the rubber band tension triggers a mechanism that suddenly throws the glider way out of adjustment. A snuffer tube holds the fuse and extinguishes it after dethermalizing to prevent ground fires. The pop-up tail is one of the safest, most

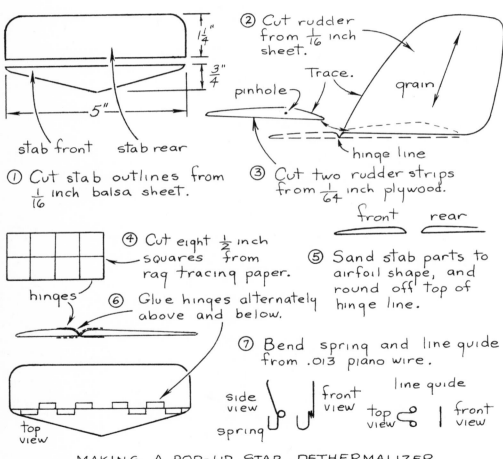

MAKING A POP-UP STAB DETHERMALIZER
(SIZES SHOWN FOR 14 INCH GLIDER)

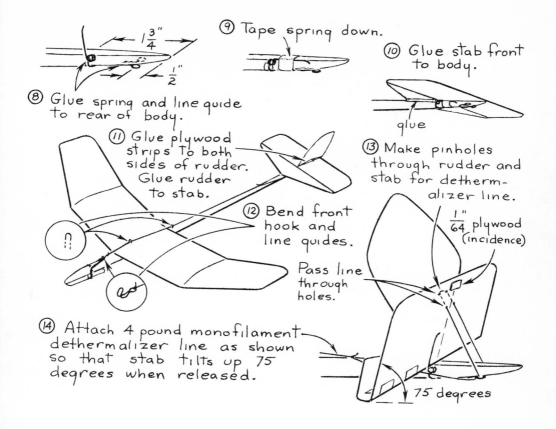

⑨ Tape spring down.

⑩ Glue stab front to body.

glue

⑧ Glue spring and line guide to rear of body.

1 3/4"   1/2"

⑪ Glue plywood strips to both sides of rudder. Glue rudder to stab.

⑫ Bend front hook and line guides.

⑬ Make pinholes through rudder and stab for dethermalizer line.

1/64" plywood (incidence)

Pass line through holes.

⑭ Attach 4 pound monofilament dethermalizer line as shown so that stab tilts up 75 degrees when released.

75 degrees

reliable, and effective dethermalizers. The detailed drawings show how it works.

Always use a longer dethermalizer fuse than required for the actual flight time, so you have time to wait for the right moment to launch into the passing thermal. When you are ready to fly and lift seems to be developing, light the fuse and wait. Keep pushing the fuse out through the open-ended snuffer tube past the rubber band, keeping the proper flight-time length ready for the instant when you want to launch.

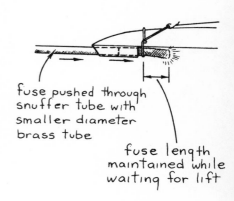

fuse pushed through snuffer tube with smaller diameter brass tube

fuse length maintained while waiting for lift

To prepare for contest flying, practice against the clock. Having a friend time you with a stopwatch is the best way, since it puts some pressure on you to perform well. It also gives you your flight times to the second, as in a contest. Flight time is measured from the instant you release the glider until the instant it touches the ground. Extra fractions of a second are dropped, and the nearest whole second is recorded. Flights are scored in seconds, so a one-minute-ten-second flight is written as seventy seconds. Total scores are also recorded in seconds.

Stopwatches are fairly expensive. If you do not have one available, you can time yourself approximately by using the sweep second hand of a wristwatch. Launch when the second hand is approaching a numbered mark. When the glider touches down, glance at the watch again and figure out the total time. With no lift present, you will be doing well if you can reach thirty to thirty-five seconds and very well if you can reach forty to forty-five seconds.

Practice flying a series of flights according to A.M.A. or German rules, and write down your times. Add up the total and fly another series, trying to better your score. If you are flying with a friend, take turns timing each other and fly a practice contest. You will be surprised at how much even this informal competition can spur you on. Go to some contests to watch experienced fliers. You will probably see that the experts can have trouble too. When you start to fly in contests, don't worry too much about the results. Just do the best you can while you continue to gain experience.

If you have a strong throwing arm, you may want to try a larger glider. Plans are

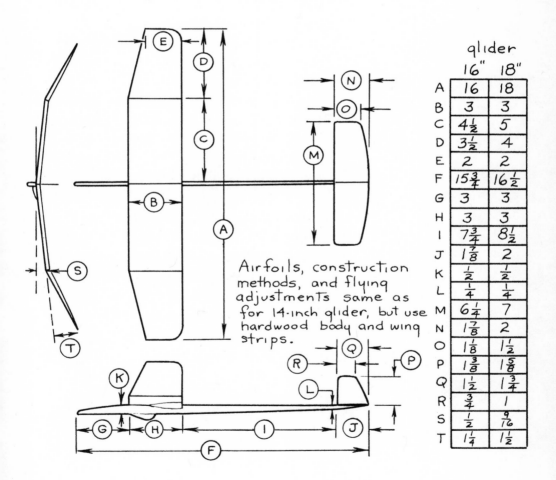

Airfoils, construction methods, and flying adjustments same as for 14-inch glider, but use hardwood body and wing strips.

	glider	
	16"	18"
A	16	18
B	3	3
C	$4\frac{1}{2}$	5
D	$3\frac{1}{2}$	4
E	2	2
F	$15\frac{3}{4}$	$16\frac{1}{2}$
G	3	3
H	3	3
I	$7\frac{3}{4}$	$8\frac{1}{2}$
J	$1\frac{7}{8}$	2
K	$\frac{1}{2}$	$\frac{1}{2}$
L	$\frac{1}{4}$	$\frac{1}{4}$
M	$6\frac{1}{4}$	7
N	$1\frac{7}{8}$	2
O	$1\frac{1}{8}$	$1\frac{1}{2}$
P	$1\frac{3}{8}$	$1\frac{5}{8}$
Q	$1\frac{1}{2}$	$1\frac{3}{4}$
R	$\frac{3}{4}$	1
S	$\frac{1}{2}$	$\frac{9}{16}$
T	$1\frac{1}{4}$	$1\frac{1}{2}$

"The climb isn't too great, but wait 'til you see the glide!"

included for one with a sixteen-inch wingspan and one with an eighteen-inch wingspan, similar to the one you have built. Try the sixteen-inch glider first. Don't assume that a larger glider will automatically give you longer flights. It will surely glide better, simply because larger wings have greater aerodynamic efficiency. But unless you can throw it fairly high, your flights may be shorter than those of a smaller, higher-climbing glider.

There are many good hand-launched glider designs. Some sources for plans and further information on design, building, and flying are listed at the end of this book. By joining the A.M.A. you can purchase books and subscribe to model magazines at reduced rates. The A.M.A. can also tell you about free-flight clubs in your area. In any club there are usually some enthusiastic hand-launched glider fliers who will gladly offer to help you with your building and flying. Talking and flying with experienced people will enable you to avoid mistakes and improve your performance.

So good luck and happy flying!

Information for Hobbyists

Sources for Supplies

(Since prices are subject to change, they are not included here. Check with the suppliers to find out current prices before ordering by mail.) Balsa wood, spruce, and other materials: SIG Manufacturing Co., 401 South Front Street, Montezuma, Iowa, 50171. "Contest" balsa can be ordered by weight and grain in grades from 4 to 6 pounds. The SIG catalog listing balsa and many other supplies can be ordered from this address. Since SIG supplies are also sold in many of the better hobby stores, write to the company to locate a dealer in your area.

Fuse rope: SIG sells fuse rope. For a cheaper supply, scout around for a source of soft (without a hard, or sized, finish) braided cotton clothesline, 3/16 or 1/4 inch thick. Make sure the rope does not have a synthetic core, since this inhibits proper burning.

Lightweight Mylar tape (for thermal streamers): F.A.I. Model Supplies, P.O. Box 9778, Phoenix, Arizona, 85068.

Telescoping Fiberglas fishing pole: (for thermal detectors, also very handy for retrieving gliders from trees) Sears, Roebuck & Co., Hunting and Fishing Catalog.

Books

The Model Aeronautic Yearbooks by Frank Zaic, Model Aeronautic Publications, Box 135, Northridge, California. The 1957–58, 1959–61, and 1964–65 *Yearbooks* contain valuable three-view drawings and articles on hand-launched gliders. These are available at some of the better hobby stores, from the A.M.A. at a discount to its members, or directly from Frank Zaic at the above address.

Magazines

These frequently have plans and articles on gliders:
American Aircraft Modeler
Flying Models
Model Airplane News
The Model Builder
N.F.F.S. Digest (available only to members of N.F.F.S.)

In addition there is an excellent article, "The Soaring Flight of Birds," by Clarence D. Cone in *Scientific American,* April 1962. This is a fine study that applies to gliders as well as birds.

Organizations

Academy of Model Aeronautics (A.M.A.), 806 Fifteenth Street, N.W., Washington, D.C. 20005.

National Free Flight Society (N.F.F.S.). Dedicated to the promotion of free-flight competition for both the beginner and the expert, N.F.F.S. publishes a digest, *Free Flight,* several times a year, as well as the annual *Symposium.* Both publications are generally highly technical and meant primarily for the expert, but the hand-launched glider articles and plans are not too difficult. Write to A.M.A. for the address of the current subscription manager.

Gliders

Here are some excellent gliders that you may want to build in the future. Plans are available in back issues of magazines, *Yearbooks,* etc., and some are available in kit form.
Bronco—18" by Tem Johnson
Curly—17" and 18" by Bill Dunwoody
Flash—18" by Dick Mathis
Polly—18" by Bill Blanchard
Square 80—22" by Jim Kutkuhn
Sweepette—19" by Lee Hines
Texas Bo-Weevil—17" by Don Chancey